MESSAGE OF THE SACRAMENTS

Monika K. Hellwig, Editor

REDEEMED CREATION
Sacramentals Today

by

Laurence F. X. Brett

Michael Glazier, Inc.
Wilmington, Delaware

First published in 1984 by Michael Glazier, Inc., 1723 Delaware Avenue, Wilmington, Delaware 19806 and distributed outside the USA and Canada by Gill and Macmillan, Ltd., Goldenbridge, Inchicore, Dublin 8

Library of Congress Catalog Card Number 84-80347
International Standard Book Number
  Message of the Sacraments series: Paper, 0-89453-226-4;|Cloth, 0-89453-280-4
  CATHOLIC SACRAMENTS
    0-89453-234-0, Paper; 0-89453-398-3, Cloth (Michael Glazier, Inc.)
    7171-1140-7 (Gill and Macmillan, Ltd.)

Cover design by Lillian Brulc

Typography by Richard Reinsmith

Printed in the United States of America

TABLE OF CONTENTS

In Memory of
ROSE MARY CHILDS
who departed from this world
on the Feast of the Presentation, 1983,
to be presented
into the temple of glory —
herself a sacramental
of the redeemed creation.

EDITOR'S PREFACE

This volume is one of the series of eight on *The Message of the Sacraments*. These volumes discuss the ritual practices and understanding and the individual sacraments of the Roman Catholic community. Each of the eight authors has set out to cover five aspects of the sacrament (or, in the first and last volumes, of the theme or issue under discussion). These are: first of all, the existential or experiential meaning of the sacrament in the context of secular human experience; what is known of the historical development of the sacrament; a theological exposition of the meaning, function and effect of the sacrament in the context of present official Catholic doctrinal positions; some pastoral reflections; and a projection of possible future developments in the practice and catechesis of the sacrament.

There is evident need of such a series of volumes to combine the established teaching and firm foundation in sacramental theology with the new situation of the post-Vatican II Church. Because the need is universal, this series is the joint effort of an international team of English-speaking authors. We have not invited any participants whose writing would need to be translated. While we hope that our series will be useful particularly to priests, permanent deacons, seminarians, and those professionally involved in sacramental and catechetical ministries, we also address ourselves confidently to the educated Catholic laity and to those outside the Roman Catholic communion who are interested in learning more about its life and thought. We have all tried to write so as to be easily understood by readers with little or no specialized preparation. We have all tried to deal with the tradition imaginatively but within the acceptable bounds of Catholic orthodoxy, in the firm conviction that that is the way in which we can be most helpful to our readers.

The Church seems to be poised today at a critical juncture in its history. Vatican II reopened long-standing questions about collegiality and participation in the life of the Church, including its sacramental actions, its doctrinal formulations and its government. The council fostered a new critical awareness and raised hopes which the Church as a vast and complicated institution cannot satisfy without much confusion, conflict and delay. This makes ours a particularly trying and often frustrating time for those most seriously interested in the life of the Church and most deeply committed to it. It seems vitally important for constructive and authentically creative community participation in the shaping of the Church's future life, that a fuller understanding of the sacraments be widely disseminated in the Catholic community. We hope that many readers will begin with the volumes in this series and let themselves be guided into further reading with the bibliographies we offer at the ends of the chapters. We hope to communicate to our readers the sober optimism with which we have undertaken the study and thereby to contribute both to renewal and to reconciliation.

Monika K. Hellwig

ACKNOWLEDGMENTS

A first acknowledgment would be to those within the Church, to all within the world, who have helped us cherish and reverence the sacredness of God's creation; however flawed, it is redeemed.

In no less a way am I indebted to Monika Hellwig, Michael Glazier and Eileen Daney Carzo. They patiently waited, and must have concluded that creation itself took a shorter time than the writing of this book. I can only hope that this "creation" stands redeemed, together with its author. To spare them further disappointment than that already experienced, I claim its failures as my own, while wishing them continued success.

Indebtedness is owed to the other contributors in this series, and an apology as well. Mine is not the depth that they possess, and I am, by nature, impatient in a world of footnotes. There is no claim to have answered any questions within this modest work; if there is any claim, it is simply to have raised additional questions. The tone throughout is one of pondering, of thinking aloud in print, and if the work appears to be a conversation with myself, then I apologize to the reader.

One failure I cannot place entirely at my door is the scarcity of material on the subject of sacramentals. All too often the subject was confined to an appendix, or an addendum. It is for this reason that suggested reading material is listed at the close of the book, and not placed after each chapter. Even within that list will be found books hard to locate, simply because they were written long before this work was undertaken. They have been included, however, because they are classics in their field. Many of them, appearing before Vatican II, were prophetic works, and lent their vision to that council.

To Chaplains Conrad Walker and John Trapold, brothers from the Lutheran and Catholic traditions respectively, I owe a debt of thanks. Their patient rearranging of schedules to meet my own allowed me the freedom and time to work on this manuscript. To Gracia Walker, who graced me with instruments, and who was more than instrumental in her kindness, a similar word of thanks is addressed.

Lastly, in the place of honor, and in treasured memory, I set my aunt, Rose Mary Childs. She became more than mother and friend to me, and to her memory this book is dedicated as but in partial repayment. When God had finished the work of creation, he rested on the seventh day; into that rest she has entered, a truly finished woman, whose approach to life and reverent appreciation for this world has colored my own. Her work done, creation's joys have deepened for her now, as have mine because of her.

INTRODUCTION

The Sunday Comics are as good a place as any to start. They are the parables of today, and often tell a larger truth than any headline. They are fables about our foibles; they enable us not to take ourselves too seriously, while providing us with serious food for thought.

A cartoonist once offered a series of panels in which a night watchman, perched atop his tower, called out the early hour of dawn. A single sentence was broken up to cover all the panels except the last:

"Five o'clock and there is an orange glow in the east
" ... it is breathtaking
" ... one senses the glory of creation
" ... and is humbled by the brilliance
" ... of the first piercing beams of dawn
" ... as it spreads majestically across the horizon
" ... another truly magnificent sunrise ... "

And then came the final panel, as the exuberant smile on the watchman's face turned into a look of shock and surprise as he added:

" ... either that or the woods are on fire!"

When it comes to this world, and how one can approach that world, there can be said to exist two distinct and opposing views. The first looks at an "orange glow," and "senses the glory of creation," humbled by its "brilliance" and grandeur; the other sees that same glow and thinks that "the woods are on fire."

The temptation exists to divide the world into two such factions, and to align ourselves with either side. The cartoon itself, however, reveals a truth that avoids such a facile division: the same person came up with both viewpoints!

There is, within the Catholic tradition, a sense of being "at home" within this world of ours, even if another part of that tradition would look at our world as "a home away from home." The basic tradition within Catholicism lies with those who find the world breathtaking, simultaneously humbled and exalted by creation's brilliance. For them, the words of Hilaire Belloc have something of the ring of a national anthem, an expansion of the "Alleluia" that marks an Easter people:

"Wherever a Catholic sun doth shine,
There's plenty of laughter and good red wine.
At least I've always found it so.
Benedicamus Domino!

"Let us bless the Lord!" That is the traditional and liturgical acclamation. It resounds within our worship when it rings true within our world. One can suspect that St. Thomas Aquinas composed the magnificent liturgy of Corpus Christi simply because he took himself to Orvieto, from which the "good red wine" is still bottled and sent out into the world. One approaches the Eucharistic food with appreciation that arises from having known hunger and thirst; only those who know hunger have an appreciation for bread, and only those who ever know thirst can appreciate what wine has to offer. But there is another side, as well, to our appreciation: only those who enjoy *good* bread can understand why it was chosen to become Body, and only those who enjoy a *good* red wine can fully fathom why the Lord, and we with him, can speak of it in terms of Blood.

An approach to sacramentals, and to sacraments therefore, rests upon one's approach to the world. The creation we view, and hopefully enjoy, speaks to us of a deeper dimension, and things as they are speak about things that are not seen. In the days before new creation began, the days before the Redeemer appeared, the prophets clearly saw the flaw which sin had introduced. Yet they were messengers of hope, and urged a return to God. In our days, when we think of the Risen One, we see creation summed up in him. If we picture him as glorious, it is only because his wounds still show. Creation itself bears semblance to him in precisely the same way, wounded yet glorious. Christ and creation both reveal God's unconditional love for the world, which John's Gospel describes in terms of "so much" love, and the gift of "his Son" (Jn 3:16). "World" and "Son" appear within the same verse, which describes what God "gave."

Yet the tension still exists between views of a world that shows splendor, and a world that is wounded. Francis of Assisi could call the earth his "brother," and the moon his "sister," yet join in the *Salve Regina* each night, singing about the earth as "a vale of tears," and our life as "this exile of ours." But the dominant memory of this humble deacon views him as the troubador of God. The gospels record that Jesus "wept" (Lk 19:41), and never once tell us that he laughed; some have pointed this out, and felt some need for explanation, while others have simply affirmed that there was no need to declare what is obvious. Luke's poignant observation, one may suppose, arises precisely as exception arises from rule.

The Foundations of an Approach to Sacramentals

Catholic thought so often turns to St. Thomas Aquinas, even as devotional thought so often turns to St. Francis of Assisi. What Francis sang in his canticle, Thomas proclaimed in his writings: *Nihil est sine voce*. Everything has its voice. "The heavens declare the glory of God, and the firmament proclaims his handiwork ... Not a word nor a discourse whose voice is not heard" (Ps 19:2,4). Creation speaks, in other words, and speaks to us of God.

This is the first truth upon which sacraments and sacramentals rest. The other lies within a part of that creation, namely the human mind. Our ability to hear what things have to say, to interpret the discourse, and perceive that a deeper reality lies underneath, this it is that allows us entrance into the world of symbols and signs. The water changed to wine at Cana. Only after Jesus "performed this first of his signs" do we learn that "his disciples believed in him" (Jn 2:11). Here was a true "wedding," as the things of earth revealed the "One who comes from heaven" (Jn 3:31), and both were inextricably joined.

The Nature of Sacrament

From the basic truth of creation (that things which are contain things which are revealed), and the basic truth that the human mind is capable of discovery and interpretation, we are led to an understanding of what sacraments are all about. Sacramental theology takes its starting point in the person of Jesus Christ, considered as *the great sacrament.* His human nature veils and reveals the divine, and both natures are one in him. From this it flows that the Church is sacrament as well, when many persons forming the one body veil and reveal Christ. It can be said that we are his other self.

Sacraments, the actions of Christ and Church, make use of things that are to veil and reveal things that are not seen. Sheer wonder at this truth, and not the simple failure to grasp that truth as theology advanced, led to some confusion between sacraments and sacramentals, as we shall see. Anchored in the Incarnation, in the fact that "the Word became flesh" (Jn 1:14), the Church came to the realization that she herself was a mystery. That very word *mysterium* would be the first, in her long and varied vocabulary, to describe what we call "sacrament."

Sacramentals Today

In the course of time, with the Church's understanding of seven sacraments, all else that concerned visible things as conveying invisible realities fell into the classification of "sacramentals." They are not the leftovers of a finished meal, the fallout of some theological explosion, but part and parcel with sacraments in our efforts to understand God and ourselves. The Editor of this series, Monika Hellwig, correctly saw the need to complete a series on "The Message of the Sacraments" with a look at sacramentals. All too often, in times past, sacramentals appeared under an appendix, an *addendum*, or were confined to a footnote or two.

They are not without their importance to the world of the sacraments, for they are important to our understanding of the world itself. Like the world, sacramentals are a world of persons, places, times and things. They speak to us about creation, and about that creation as redeemed. What has value has new and deeper value now, and such is our faith.

The woods are not "on fire." One can sense the "glory of creation." Any sunrise should be called "truly magnificent," and not just the start of another day.

PART ONE

AN APPROACH TO SACRAMENTALS

The "word of the Lord" came to Jeremiah in the form of a question, asking "What do you see?" "A branch of the watching tree," came the reply, and the Lord remarked that the youth saw well, "for I am watching to fulfill my word." In the call to be a prophet (Jer 1:4-12), Jeremiah admitted that he did not know how to speak, but learned that he knew how to see.

The almond tree spoke to him. It was the first to put forth its blossoms, as though it had "kept watch" throughout the winter, and had never slept at all. He saw the tree, and a challenge by "the word of the Lord" blossomed into significance for him, and something of God's nature was perceived.

As we approach the subject of sacramentals, our human experiences must be considered first (Chapter 1), for this world of ours is not a mere concept, but the realm in which we see, and hear, and taste and touch. Through our senses we make sense of it. One wonders whether "salvation" would ever have come to Zacchaeus' house had he never climbed a tree.

Then we must turn attention to the sacred word, for in that word Paul confirms "that whatever can be known about God is clear," and "recognized through the things he has made" (Rom 1:19,20). "Invisible realities" have become "visible," he adds, providing the very language whereby we speak of sacrament and sacramental alike. In Chapter 2, we shall consider this "sacred world."

And lastly, in Chapter 3, we move to a consideration of the sacramentals as they have been used throughout the history of the Church. For the Church seeks not only to ponder the word it has received, but to do the very things which Jesus, Word-made-flesh, had done.

Things done by others spoke to him, even in his parables. He could notice how the Pharisee prayed "with head unbowed," or how the tax-collector "kept his distance . . . and beat his breast." And even though Jesus gave them words to say, as he spoke his story, their actions had said it all (Lk 18:9-14).

And when he had finished washing his disciples' feet, a gesture that moves and embarrasses us at the same time, he had a question to ask: "Do you understand what I just *did* for you?" (Jn 13:12). (It seems that God is always asking questions, whether about watching-trees or washings.) In every sacramental, as in every sacrament, that same question remains to be answered. Do we understand what he just *did* for us?

With a touch he healed (Mk 1:41), and sometimes even "the tassel on his cloak" was sufficient for a cure (Lk 8:44). Early in his gospel-story, Mark speaks of "a leper" who approached Jesus, "kneeling down as he addressed him" (Mk 1:40), and finding healing, again with a touch.

For Catholic thought, things remain the same, and ours is a world of gesture and movement, of posture and prayer, of time and place and persons. Ours is a sacramental world, and even the world itself a "sacramental," for we speak, in faith, about "the life of the world to come." To that phrase we add "Amen," not merely because the Creed ends there, but because we affirm its value.

And so we begin with "an approach to sacramentals," as they have been perceived, and even as they have been misperceived.

CHAPTER I

SACRAMENTALS AND HUMAN EXPERIENCE

When *Time* magazine looked back over the first sixty years of its history, it devoted one section to what it termed "Triumphs of the Spirit." As it took note of "how history responds to ideas and yearnings," it paid special attention to the Second Vatican Council, and described how "the church threw itself open to risk." For *Time* magazine, at least, Vatican II was "a force that seized the mind of the Roman Catholic Church and carried it across centuries, from the 13th to the 20th."

In the eyes of the world, the Church threw open its windows and faced the world. Symbolic of that approach is the document addressed to the world, the *Pastoral Constitution on the Church in the Modern World*. Since most official documents are known by their opening words, that constitution is best known as *Gaudium et Spes*, "Joy and Hope." Even the very title bespeaks a vision.

Nestled within those opening words, in which the Church calls "the hopes and joys, grief and anguish of the people of our time" its very own, is a statement that is profound in its simplicity and obvious truth. The Church put itself officially on record as declaring:

"For the followers of Christ, nothing genuinely human fails to find an echo in their hearts."

In any approach to sacramentals, that statement must form a starting-point. In a very real way, sacramentals are "echoes" of all that is "genuinely human." It is within the world of human experience that one searches for the meaning of sacred signs and symbols. What is valid in that experience finds revalidation in the experience of God that lies at the heart of Catholic life and worship.

The same conciliar document affirms that the human person is "a unity," and "through bodily condition sums up all the elements of the material world" (Art 14). In other words, the human being is *a part* of this world, and never *apart* from it. From the first moments of our lives we are discoverers of the rest of creation. We explore the terrain that already lies before us, mark our own paths or follow a course already charted, at least in part, and in the process discover much about ourselves.

For the child that ever remains within us, the world becomes a playroom, and for the adult that allegedly emerges, it must be a workroom. But the world is more than that; it is schoolroom and storeroom. We mine its riches and cherish its treasures, and at the same time we are nourished, sustained, educated and formed by it. For the child, the commonplace is extraordinary and fascinating; and only when we have put it to practical use, or tired of it, or robbed it of its meaning, does it ever revert to being ordinary once again.

It is commonly agreed, among those who study the mind and its ways with the world, that the child does remain within us, and our adult selves form the outward appearance. How children react to things reveals what our approach to the world is, or at least can be. The child first sees and feels, and once the eyes can fix upon an object, the child's world becomes one of reaching out to touch, thereby learning in a new way. Long before the child can name a toy, and ask for it, that object has been seen, felt, manipulated and, all too often, tasted.

Always, as the object is approached, there is a sense of mystery. The child who opens a present on Christmas Day, it is observed, will spend more time with the wrappings than with the gift itself, and parents are often found to remark that they could have given the child an empty box. Perhaps the fascination lies in the hope that more is to be discovered, and that things are meant to contain other things. It could be said that adults who open their gifts carefully, outwardly offering the pragmatic view that the wrappings can be used again, are simply preserving something of the mystery.

What we do, whether as children or adults, reveals what we are. Actions express our being at its deepest level. We make use of words, but they apply to the world of concepts. The more immediate expression is an action or a reaction, a gesture or a movement of some type. Actions do speak more loudly than words, and if words express our thoughts, deeds express our deepest selves.

Plato was right when he observed that the soul "grows wings" whenever it beholds a value. The child constantly asks "What?," and "Why?" It is not mere curiosity, but a search for values, and the child "grows wings," so to speak. As Genesis recounts the "childhood" of Adam, we find that all the birds and beasts were brought before him, and he "gave names" to them all. That's precisely what we do with our countless questions; we examine the world, and organize it for ourelves. If none of the creatures "was a suitable partner" for Adam, the very search for values represents our willingness to enter into a partnership with the world, and to define ourselves in the process.

As each person "gives names" to the things of earth, something of the child in us, the Adam in us, is at work. The giving of names represents the assigning of values that are already perceived, or await development. It is this truth that establishes what we might call "human sacramentals." The elements of the world speak for themselves, sometimes as clearly as we do when we speak their names.

Things, places, times, gestures, even other persons, already have their meaning. When they become more meaningful to us, they become invested with deeper meaning.

Sometimes we add a meaning that the object never possessed, and that can be a risky business; but even that process reveals that the search for symbols is a very human thing. The fact that dubious meanings were attached to some sacramentals of the Church only proves that the "genuinely human" found its echo there as well.

Times and Seasons

Even as Genesis recounted the stories about creation, it did so with the marking of "days," the passing of time. It is a fascination that left its stamp on human inventiveness, from grains of sand shifting downward in an hourglass to those alarm clocks that flash their digital numbers across a ceiling, allowing time to be observed without any effort on our part. The fascination continued to be spelled out with bells and chimes to mark even the quarters of an hour, or the glockenspiels, with their mechanical figures that enact a scene from history.

For every individual, there are days that are special. They mark the milestones of our rites of passage through life, measurements of where we were, and guides to where we hope to be. We remember and celebrate the day of our birth, and do so with appropriate symbols made acceptable by common use; the cake, with its candles, identifies the day, as do the gifts and the singing of a song. For the more seasonably trained among us, the day is also marked with a gift that says "thank you" to the parents who gave us life.

The days that are important to us, invested with meaning for ourselves and those close to us, each have their symbol. Such signs accompany and intensify the symbolic day itself. Graduation has its printed scroll and its traditional attire, including the "mortar-board" that startled parents in ancient Greece, when first used, to remind them that what their children learned would be relearned in human labor. Wedding anniversaries are marked each year with gifts that increase in value, from paper to precious gems, and even that tradition says something about a marriage that deepens in appreciation with the passing of years.

In our individual lives, apart from those days that are observed by each of us alike, there are days that speak only to us. The day we met a special person in our lives, or the first-day we occupied a new home, or the day when someone close to us died — all are special, invested with significance.

As members of society, days and seasons have their own importance in the life of a city or a nation. Red Square in Moscow, on October 17th, is no less afloat with banners than any town square in American on the 4th of July. Such days declare our identity as a nation, however opposite one people may be to another in their political identity.

In a word, there are days that are not days at all, but festivals of the human spirit. Even the frivolous has its right to celebration, and Ground Hog Day will make headlines even if the furry little creature fails to emerge. There are seasons to the soul, sublime and ridiculous, and this "genuinely human" observance finds its echo in the Feasts and Solemnities of the Church's Year.

Space and Places

It has also been observed that we are territorial animals, and the dimension of space says something about who we are. Even as Acts reports the first proclamations of Jesus as "the Messiah," it does so in terms of Jesus as "the Nazorean" (Acts 2:22). After all the geographical references in the opening two chapters, Matthew's Gospel offers a final "title" for Jesus, declaring that he was "called a Nazorean" (Mt 2:23). Only after that does the ministry of Jesus begin to be told.

Where we are defines *who* we are to a great extent. We constantly mark our territory as our very own, and home-decorators make their living by assuring owners that any given room will express their personalities. Even without designers to help us, we do quite well for ourselves, and can find meaning in what someone else wrongly perceives to be "clutter."

As did Adam when the birds and beasts were summoned before him, we give "names" to places, some prosaic, others poetic. Like children looking at moving clouds, we look for patterns on the face of a mountain, or else carve out a Mt. Rushmore. To a lesser degree we simply leave initials or a name, and some of us might secretly hope that the climber, when she or he reaches the summit, will find that someone else was there before, and left a name and a date.

Spaces become places, and places have a way of becoming special, not only to individuals, but to entire nations as well. We connect them with persons and events, and fix them in our minds so that we are never really distant. It is a "genuinely human" thing to do, and finds its echo in our churches, to which we give names that have meaning, and in our cemeteries, where names and dates have every right to appear.

Gesture and Movement

It is within the world of touch and movement that the human person speaks most eloquently, even when words are used. "Hello" can be an ordinary greeting, until the hand is extended, or the shoulder patted. "Goodbye" cannot be spoken at times, and even that fact is expressed in tightened lips that betray our unwillingness to even speak. And at times of grief, when words fail us, as they so often do, an embrace or a tear will say it all.

At times when words are meant to fail, a gesture is all that is needed. Angry words could never express what a silence can convey. One had no need to know what words were exchanged between Pope John Paul II and his assailant. The arms of the Pontiff around the would-be assassin's neck tells the story; so does the gesture that was returned, the traditional Moslem sign of respect, when one's forehead touches the hand of someone who is esteemed.

A nod of the head has its own meanings, as does the holding of hands. Each culture is steeped in signs that are performed, and those gestures are a language complete and entire of themselves. Each nation makes use of postures and movements rightly understood as their own, and the salutes of a soldier, as well as a hand held over the heart, are only different ways of saying the same thing.

Our individual gestures have their echo in the sign of the cross, or a genuflection, even if the knee never actually touches the floor. Together we sit and stand within our worship, as we do at civic functions, signs of respect or attentiveness.

The movement of a group finds its echo in what the Church calls its processions. They are solemn parades, but parades nonetheless. Cross and candles need not precede, and people need not march in step, as when we form queues for the Holy Communion. But the very movement signifies that we are a pilgrim people, and there is an exodus, a passing over that is taking place, even without water like a wall to the right and to the left of us.

Clothing and Insignia

Clothing may not make the person, but however essential to human life, clothing is costume, and others can identify us by what we wear. We "dress" for the everyday world, and "dress up" for times that are special. Even uniforms are hardly "uniform," for while the wearers are *identical* in appearance, they are somewhat *identified*, and relate to that identity.

The garb of everyday has often become specialized, and what was once practical necessity often became a sign of one's profession. The frock that scientists use has become standard clothing for doctors; the ordinary dress of the day passed on unchanged, and religious women found themselves in the 20th century looking exactly as they did centuries ago.

What Gerard Manley Hopkins called "their tackle, gear and trim" often became not merely tools of the trade, but symbols of the profession. The measuring tape of tailors and the stethoscope of interns is as much a badge as any worn by soldiers, or a sash like those which ambassadors are given.

The "genuinely human" found its echo in the vestments

worn at liturgies, and the insignia of office, such as miter and staff. Such items were not merely borrowed by the Church, but bestowed upon it by emperors and magistrates.

And with such things as clothing and insignia, all that pertains to cloth entered the Church as well. The very textures and colors we use have something to say, even if only our inability to match things well. Textures spoke to the Church; the rough bespoke penitence, and the rare was given to adorn the most precious things, altar and ciboriums. If, as happened, symbols were added to symbols, so that cloth became hidden beneath them, that too is not without a lesson. Clothing was meant to speak for itself, and when not allowed to speak its own truth, it at least had meaning forced upon it.

Things

If any one element of the world can be called a sacramental, as most of us define the term, then it would be an object that has, or receives, special meaning. A seashell recalls a place and a time that will be different when vacation is over. An item, even one that's broken, cannot be tossed away when it is overlaid with memories. What appears to be a knick-knack for someone else may represent a treasure to us.

If everyone has a drawer into which such things find their resting place, the nation itself is not without its "attic," a museum for things to be mused, and for things that amuse. A history is recounted in artifacts that are preserved, and we are unwilling to sustain loss at any level.

What portraits did in ages past is now accomplished by photographs, even if we would prefer that nobody should ever see them. It is a "genuinely human" thing to do, this capturing of memories, this tribute to those we love, or those we love who are distant from us. Whether it be in the world of space, or the world of time, photos bridge a distance, and draw the world closer to us.

No nation is without its monuments, the statues of its

leaders and heroes, and settings to lend them prominence. The same thing applies to our churches, where leaders and heroes of the faith are represented with a semblance of that glory which they now share, and which lies hidden from our sight. Statues and icons present, to the eyes of faith, the memories of those who loved God, and whose lives challenge our own. For persons, no less than places or things, are special to us, and very special to God.

In the final analysis we are not unlike Adam, symbol of us all. Our bodies are of the earth, and the breath within comes from God's own breath. There is "a unity" about us, and we can no more conceive of things divine without the things of earth than we can sustain our lives by concepts alone, and never taste bread, or drink wine.

Things reveal themselves to us, and we to them, and the process is sacramental. There is no world of difference between the ways of the world and the ways of the Church. In the way we accept persons and places, times and things, gestures and movements and all the elements of earth, we trace what is important in the realm of grace.

Ours is a world of symbols and values; and signs, whether sacred or profane, present themselves in many dimensions. Signs *remember* the past, *declare* a present truth, *oblige* us in an ongoing way, and *foresee* the future.

Each sacramental is a sign that *remembers*, as events are recalled with all their attendant emotions. Days and seasons do this in a way that gestures cannot fully do but memories are attached to both, as indeed to all the elements of our world.

Each sacramental is a sign that *declares*, and if the statement seems directed only to us, or understood by others as well, it is a statement nonetheless. Clothes do this, but not in such a way that places or objects are prevented from having their say.

Each sacramental is a sign that *obliges*, for anniversaries force us to renew our commitment, and a birthday makes us take stock of our origins, the paths we have taken so far, and the roads yet to be travelled. With persons, such obligation is essential, but there is also a commitment to the earth, and to the universe in which we live, as well as a commitment to one another.

Each sacramental is a sign that *foresees*, for the past is parent to the present, and to the future as well. A seed is more than a seed, as the Lord Jesus himself knew full well, when he held a mustard-seed in his hands and spoke to his disciples about what they would become.

Remembrance, declaration, obligation and promise — all are present in the world of which we are a part. That the same elements should be present in sacraments and sacramentals should not take us by surprise. "For the followers of Christ, nothing genuinely human fails to find an echo in their hearts."

Perhaps we should say, nothing genuinely sacred fails to find its echo in the world, and in the human experience which interprets that world.

CHAPTER II

SACRED WORD, SACRED WORLD

The God who reveals himself in sacred scripture, to which we give the name "Word of God," does so not by words alone, but in events in which creation was intimately involved. Signs and symbols abound, and *word* is partner to *deed*. As Genesis tells the story, a *word* was spoken and a *deed* emerged, and as John continues the story, the *word* took *flesh*. Only then could the evangelist say, "we have *seen* his glory" (Jn 1:14).

There is nothing in the world of human experience that does not find its place in the sacred experience narrated by the Bible. The initiative is God's from start to finish, and God's choosing is without constraint. He chose to speak to the world his word had formed, and clothed that word in ways to which the world itself would lend expression. In the self-revelation of God to his creation, all the elements of earth were summoned into play — places, seasons, things common and rare, gestures and movement aplenty, and persons, particularly one person, in whom the fullness of Godhead became manifest in a way that still causes wonder and awe.

The Creation

Perhaps that is the reason why the sacred word begins with creation itself, a sign of creation's even larger role with the passing of time. Time itself is "sacramentalized," and each "day" marked with the emergence of things that never were. Given our understanding of the Church's sacramentals, the end of the first story of creation (Gn 1:3) relates that "God *blessed* the seventh day and made it *holy*," something the Church has done as she anchored herself in history.

Places, creatures, symbols, clothing — all are present in these first eleven chapters of Genesis. Eden and serpents and "fiery revolving sword" all speak on their own. Scripture always speaks to the imagination, providing images that remain long after the word, whether read or spoken, has passed. It is this vivid imagery that validates our use of sacramentals together with the truth that God chose the things of the world to address the world.

From the prehistory of creation, with all its subsequent tragedies of Fall and flood, of bricks and Babel, one single, still creative word emerges: "God looked at everything he had made, and he found it very good" (Gn 1:31). In time, as the story continues to unfold, the very *good* would become very *holy*. If the axiom holds true that the "law of praying is the law of believing," then the Church's own prayer best offers commentary upon creation:

> "Almighty and ever-present Father,
> your watchful care reaches from end to end
> and orders all things in such power
> that even the tensions and tragedies of sin
> cannot frustrate your loving plans."
> (Roman Sacramentary, 2nd Sunday of year.)

That opening collect continues by asking: "help us to embrace your will ... and follow your call." As scripture continues to outline salvation's history, we discover that such was God's loving purpose all along. Calls were issued, and help provided, in order to restore to the world the goodness that God noticed at its beginning.

A People's History

The prehistory of Genesis 1-11 sets the stage for salvation's history, which commences with the call to Abram. As prehistory ends, with the attempt to build a tower at Babel, and thus "make a name" for its builders, we are prepared to hear that Abram will receive "a great name." The call seems to come out of nowhere, as when creation began, and the word that is spoken to Abram is a creative word. It calls him into being.

Abram himself will be "a blessing," and the nations of the world will "find blessing" in him (Gn 12:2,3). The call is a *word*, but the response was a *deed*. "Abram went as the Lord directed him" (Gn 12:4). Simply that, and nothing more. No response given save to act; no words recorded, merely the doing of a deed.

From that moment on, the story of a people will be told, countless calls issued, and similar responses given. The word calls for a deed, and is completed thereby. Abram's response will become the pattern of his descendants' replies. His gestures will inform Israel's very worship of God, as when the Lord appeared at Mamre, and we find Abraham "bowing to the ground" (Gn 18:2).

As one moves further along, and encounters the God who intervened in history, similar gestures will be repeated. At Horeb, with fire and wind to symbolize his presence, God will command Moses to remove his sandals, for "the place ... is holy ground" (Ex 3:5). After the deliverance from Egypt, when Moses again approached "the mountain," on the morning of "the third day," Sinai was "wrapped in smoke," and "the trumpet blasts grew louder and louder." All the while, "Moses was *speaking*," while "God was *answering* him with thunder" (Ex 16:16-19). Words are spoken, and the elements of earth form God's reply.

Throughout the history of that chosen people, words and deeds will be repeated, like versicle and response, in a liturgy of continued covenant. The things of earth will have their say, and will even speak on God's behalf.

And as the story continues, words and deeds will both

address themselves to the truth of a people called to be holy, called to be *wholly* themselves, as were male and female when God created them "in his image."

Places will have their say, and be given "names" that are still in use, adopted by cities in other lands and cultures. Massah and Meribah will spark remembrance of failure, as will Jerusalem. Bethlehem, the city of David, despite its small size, will grow in importance, until, in the gospel story, it becomes "no means least" among the cities of Judah (Mt 2:6).

Seasons and times will have their say, marking the weekly arrival of the day of rest, which God had already "blessed" when creation was finished, and announcing times of festival and atonement. In the Wisdom literature, Ecclesiastes would mark "an appointed time for everything, and for every affair under the heavens" (Ecc 3:1).

Persons will have importance in their own right, and be given names with greater significance. Abram would be called Abraham (great father), his name thereby indicating the fulfillment of a promise. And Isaiah, having requested that King Ahaz seek "a sign," offers a sign of God's own choosing, a child with the name "Emmanuel," and all that that name has come to signify.

Objects will assume larger identities. The "rock" from which Moses obtained water will emerge in rabbinic tradition as a rock that followed God's people; it will enter the scriptures again, and receive new meaning, as Paul refers to this "rock that was following them" with a startling identification, and declares that "the rock was Christ" (1 Cor 10:4). Israel would call upon God as "the rock" of their salvation in its Psalms, and Isaiah, when speaking of Abraham, would declare: "Look to the rock from which you were hewn" (Is 51:1). That same name, or title, would be given to Simon, and "upon this rock" the Church would be founded (Mt 16:18). A single word, a single symbol, would be applied and reapplied, and images borrowed to tell a truth in many ways.

Music was allowed to speak, and does so still within the Psalms, even if the notes have not been provided. They invoke the name of God, and each metaphor summons up an earthly reality to designate the divine majesty: God is "shield" and "just judge" (Ps 7), "alloted portion and cup" (Ps 16), a "rock, and a fortress" (Ps 18),"shepherd" (Ps 23) and "light" (Ps 27), and "a stronghold" with "pinions" to cover one, and "wings" for refuge (Ps 91).

And then, in the final song, "everything that has breath" joins in his praises, together with an orchestra of instruments — trumpets, lyres and harps, strings and pipe, and cymbals that sound, together with louder ones that clash.

In a word, "everything" that was "genuinely human" was pressed into service. At each turning of the story, as God continually sought to have what he saw as "very good" become "holy" as he was holy, the elements of creation took their proper and assigned roles.

Even the failures continue the language of sign and symbol, as the prophets, those who spoke on God's behalf, uttered the call to be a holy people.

Isaiah would speak of Ephraim as a "majestic garland" even as he described "the fading blooms" (Is 28:1), and that same book would picture Jerusalem as "a mother" (66:9), with "abundant breasts" to nourish her children (66:11).

Jeremiah, called "a fortified city, à pillar of iron, a wall of brass" (Jer 1:18), will speak of God's own "word" and say it is "like fire," and "like a hammer shattering rocks" (Jer 23:29).

And Ezekiel, whose vision of "dry bones" still startles our imagination, would confront the separate nations, Judah and Israel, with a striking image of unity. He would pick up "two sticks," join them together in his hand, and declare in God's name that Judah and Israel "shall be one in my hand" (Ez 37).

As the story draws to its partial close, and prophets continued to speak until prophets were no more, Hosea is given a strange command, and told to "take a harlot wife" (Hos 1:2) because "the land" which held, and fulfilled, a promise had "given itself to harlotry." His wife would become a symbol of a people that had failed to follow their Lord. It is but prelude to the promise Hosea was soon to make, in which the Lord declares that he will "espouse" his people "in love and in mercy" (Hos 2:21).

It is a curious imagery, which tells of a God who could not renounce Israel any more than Hosea could renounce an unfaithful wife whom he loved. The Lord, whom the prophet describes as "one who roars like a lion," would, within the same statement (Ch 11) speak of God's burning love for his people, whom God had "fostered like one who raises an infant to his cheeks" (11:4).

In creation, and in the history of God's chosen ones, all the elements of this world of ours were used to tell God's story. The tensions and tragedies of sin would not frustrate his plan. The world that was "very good" was used to call a people to become "holy." Sacramentals abound within the Hebrew Scriptures, born not only of human experience, but divine as well. Two worlds mingle within those pages, the sacred and the profane, and both were to become commingled in the word and deed that is Christ.

New Testament

The promise, and the burning love, that so fill the Law, the Writings and the Prophets, would reach their fulfillment in the gift that proved how "God so loved the world" (Jn 3:16). It is not without tremendous significance that John's Gospel opens with the same words that all of scripture does, "In the beginning." The one "through whom the world was made" was "in the world," and "made his dwelling among us" (Jn 1:10, 14).

Catholic faith has constantly affirmed the truth of the Incarnation that took place "in the fullness of time" (Gal 4:4). In him, as Thomas Aquinas would observe, "*gesta Verbi verba sunt*," and "the deeds of the Word" were truly "words," from which one truly learns. The "God who spoke in fragmentary ways" has "spoken to us through his Son," the one "through whom he first created the universe" (Heb 1:1,2). Or, as the theologians have never failed to point out,

Christ is the "Great Sacrament." Human nature veils the divine, and reveals it at the same time.

Places and times, gestures and movements, persons and things, all will continue to be used as the story of a people becomes the story of a person, who is "the reflection of his Father's glory" (Heb 1:4), the "exact representation" of his being. In him, who shares our status as creature, the Creator is present to creation.

As Jesus walked among us, all the elements of creation would be put at the service of the word. Ordinary things would be vested with extraordinary meaning — mustard seed and leaven, weeds and wheat, lamps with and without their oil, fig trees and coins, specks of dust and mountains, as well as the very ones who followed him, and later proclaimed him Lord.

In page after page the sacred images flow, including stones that had been rejected, and living stones, used to describe the Lord and his Church. At his hands, the things of earth were allowed to speak, and as his message went out to the ends of the earth, they spoke, and continue to speak.

"In him everything continues in being," and by means of him "everything, both on earth and in the heavens" is reconciled to God, achieved "through the blood of his cross" (Col 1:17,20).

The sacraments tell the rest of the story, for it continues still, and so do the sacramentals as well. They speak of "the mystery, the plan ... to bring all things in the heavens and on earth into one under Christ's headship" (Eph 1:9,10), and of "the church which is his body, the fullness of him who fills the universe in all its parts" (Eph 1:23).

Even if the mystery took centuries to fathom, or was only partially understood, that loving plan lies at the heart of the Church's life and worship. Creation and Incarnation, the Paschal Mystery, and that mystery shared under sacred signs — these truths reveal a sacred world, disclosed in a sacred word, and lying at the heart of sacramentals, which can never be considered trivial, or lacking in significance.

CHAPTER III

DEVELOPMENT OF SACRAMENTALS

It is not a difficult task to pass from consideration of the sacred word to look at the development of sacramentals within the Church's life. Word and deed combine, and sacraments result; words and elements are joined, and sacramentals are constituted. The one reinforces the other, as Augustine was to point out, and each enlightens the other, deepening its meaning. Deeds express what words do, if only in a different way.

As the Church began her existence, the religion and practices of Judaism formed the matrix. God had revealed himself to Israel through things and events; those who came to know him in Christ could do no less as they revealed their faith in him. The God of creation is known in his creation, and yet is not confused with it, and the Hebrew Scriptures, whatever images it may employ, never confuses the two.

Born within the environment that was Israel's expression of faith, Jesus and his disciples were accustomed to approach God as Judaism did. Passover was observed, with all its attendant ritual and wording, and the disciples are shown baptizing early in the ministry of Jesus (Jn 4:2), and travelling with their Master to keep the festivals at Jerusalem.

Long before the words of Jesus came to be passed on and finally recorded, his deeds were established as the pattern of life and worship for those who came to believe in him. It is while the New Testament is being written that the liturgy of the Church was already taking shape. Hymns and canticles were sung, fragments of which became embedded within epistles and Revelation. Missionaries were sent forth after prayer and the laying on of hands, and the letter of James could mention the anointing with oil for those who were sick.

One searches in vain for a treatise on the worship of the early Church within the New Testament, and the picture that does emerge is fragmentary at best. The very terms we use so familiarly are not categorized therein, and are present only in seed. Precise definitions cannot be found within the writings of Paul or James, and mention of the sacraments seems confined to answering disputes that had arisen, or problems that called for attention.

As for the history of sacramentals, it is intricately woven with the development of the sacraments, or, more precisely, the Church's understanding of the sacraments. As the Church grew out of its Jewish matrix, and encountered cultures far different from earliest days, the liturgy of the Church would grow and expand. Language and ways of thought would be employed, new modes of expression formulated, and various customs "baptized," so to speak, as the worship of the Church continued to be the vibrant experience that marked those early centuries.

What Paul could call "the table of the Lord" (1 Cor 10:21) would soon be referred to as an altar. What was presented on that table, as on the altar of today, was the same reality, however. Baptism came to be known as "enlightenment," but water was poured, and the traditional words were spoken, and new life conferred, as is the case today.

The Church was busy carrying on its life, and if precise definitions were not given, it was because none were expected or demanded by others; those within the Church knew of what they spoke and believed.

For close to a thousand years, from days that saw a Church persecuted to days that saw her flourish, the sacraments were acted and received, as were the sacramentals. In fact, there was no precise agreement as to the number of sacraments, and how they operated was something that was experienced rather than explained. Names were given, but they lent themselves to sacrament and sacramental alike.

In the world where Platonic philosophy served as guide to thought, even within the Church, the world was perceived as but "a shadow" of deeper realities that lay beneath. Such thought could look at "yearly or monthly feasts," and agree with the author of Colossians that "these were but a shadow of things to come" (Col 2:17). The practices of Jewish religion often lent themselves to the explanation of Christian sacraments, and circumcision could be seen as a rite that foreshadowed baptism, all the more readily so since Passover had already colored the meal that was Holy Eucharist.

Sacraments came to be known as "mysteries," and the word which once, in the singular, was used to describe God's hidden plan for salvation, now became a term to imply that unseen grace was conferred in rites that appealed to our senses.

In the Latin-speaking world, the word used for these "mysteries" was *sacramentum*. Originally it meant an oath, such as soldiers took upon entering military service, or a pledge of payment, deposited by a party in a law suit. Christian authors like Cyprian and Tertullian used it to describe a solemn obligation, but they also employed it to describe what we mean by "sacrament," and as such it has passed into general usage within the Church.

For the thousand years or so that it took to come to precise definitions for the sacraments, any discussion of sacramentals was but a small part of a greater issue. Saint Augustine, who left his trace in presenting us with such phrases as "visible form" and "invisible grace," included several sacramentals among the sacraments themselves. For him, the font of baptism, and the giving of salt during that ceremony, as well as ashes, the Lord's Prayer and Easter Sunday were sacraments. Centuries would pass before a definition of how "invisible grace" could be given by "visible forms" would be arrived at, but the mystery of God's gift of self in visible signs was still experienced, and still caused wonder.

Not until the number and nature of the sacraments were determined could any theology about sacramentals make its own appearance. As late as the 12th century, Hugh of St. Victor would still consider ashes and holy water, together with sacred vessels and vestments, as "sacraments" and "lesser sacraments." In that same century, Peter the Lombard would list the "seven sacraments of the New Law," and from this point on sacramentals at last could be considered in and of themselves.

Sacramentals Until Now

The work of theologians began to address itself to the nature and number of sacramentals in the 13th century. With the same delight that they took in asking, "How many angels can dance on the head of a pin?" (without first asking, "How many angels can dance?"), they tackled the world of sacramentals, defining and dividing, but always taking into consideration that sacramentals "resembled the sacraments in some way."

This remained the classic definition, and by the addition of a phrase ("used by the church to obtain certain effects, usually of a spiritual kind, through her intercession"), one arrives at the description that entered the Code of Canon Law (in force until Advent of 1983). Still, the lists differed as to what should be considered sacramentals. Sprinkling with holy water, and the various "blessings" of the Church, always appeared on such lists. To them, some would add the Invocation of the name of Jesus, the eating of blessed bread, public confession of sins (apart from the sacrament of Reconciliation), and almsgiving; others would include the

Sign of the Cross, Exorcisms and Ritual Anointings (such as those within the sacrament of Baptism).

Care was always given that sacramentals, however closely they resemble the sacraments, should never be confused with those sacraments. Both are outward signs, and both convey a deeper reality.

Until the present, the tendency was to restrict the concept of a sacramental, and to exclude some rites of the Church (such as the Divine Office, or Liturgy of the Hours) from any enumeration. Quite simply, sacramentals have been seen as falling into two categories, *objects* and *actions*.

Sacred objects (holy water, blessed candles, ashes and the like) are those that result from the Church's activity and prayer;

Sacred actions are those rites, those very actions, which pass with the moment they take place. They are actions which —

constitute a person, place or thing for God's use, and set it aside for his purposes;

call down God's blessing upon persons, places or things; or,

cast out any evil influence from persons, places or things (Exorcisms).

Vatican II and Sacramentals

With the above understanding of what constitutes a sacramental, the Second Vatican Council, as it addressed the reform of the Church's liturgy, referred to sacramentals several times. In her *Constitution on the Sacred Liturgy*, we find these statements:

> "Holy Mother Church has instituted sacramentals. These are sacred signs which bear a resemblance to the sacraments. They signify effects, particularly of a spiritual nature, which are obtained through the Church's intercession. By them we are disposed to receive the chief effects of the sacraments, and various occasions of life are rendered holy" (Art 60).

"The liturgy of the sacraments and sacramentals sanctifies almost every event in the lives of the faithful with the divine grace that flows from the paschal mystery of Christ. From this source all sacraments and sacramentals draw their power. There is scarcely any proper use of material things which cannot thus be directed toward the sanctification of persons and the praise of God"(Art 61).

Notice those elements which provide a sense of definition to sacramentals:

First, they are "sacred signs," and as such they bear a resemblance to the sacraments. Theologians had always exercised caution, once the nature and number of sacraments was finally determined, not to revert back to the days when a confusion existed between the two. Their attention was focused on the "how" involved in conferring grace, and an effect of that study was to lessen the importance of sacramentals. The conciliar document simply states that they "bear a resemblance" to the sacraments, thus restoring sacramentals to their proper status as signs of the sacred.

Second, they draw their origin and strength from the Paschal Mystery, the death-and-rising of the Lord Jesus. This event has been seen as a "new creation," a vision that comes to its highest point in that most remarkable of the New Testament writings, the Book of Revelation. It describes "new heavens and a new earth," a "new Jerusalem;" and one hears, from "the One who sat on the throne," these words: "See, I make all things new!" (Rev 21:1,2,5).

Third, they involve the proper use of material things, a reverence for created things, in other words. It is a sentiment closely allied to the attitude expressed in *Gaudium et Spes* concerning the "genuinely human" that finds its "echo" in the Church.

The thrust of Vatican II, independent of its view of sacraments and sacramentals, addresses our approach to both. An openness to the world is perceived by many to have been its most salient feature, especially to those who view the Church from the outside. A second characteristic is the reverent approach to the scriptures, with hundreds upon hundreds of quotations and references from the Bible to lend words to the wording of conciliar documents. The decrees concerning the liturgy speak of "the treasures of the Bible," which are to be "opened up more lavishly so that a richer fare may be provided for the faithful at the table of God's Word" (Art 51). The council did precisely that in the use of scripture, the *Decree on Revelation*, and in the many efforts to promote biblical studies that have flourished as a result of the Council.

In discussing sacramentals, the Council admitted that "certain features have rendered the purpose and nature of sacramentals far from clear to the people of today" and that "changes are needed" (Art 62). Calling for "changes to adapt them to present needs," (a work undertaken in the revision of the Ritual, for example), the thrust of Vatican II had its part to play. A conciliar approach that looks at word and world will guide the future use of sacramentals, and enhance their value.

REDEEMED CREATION

One could readily trace a "theology" of creation from the sacred texts. A view of the world as a place of travail could equally be presented. Texts must be placed in context, and never made into pretexts; using the scriptures wrongly, by relating unconnected passages indiscriminately, or by reading into them to produce "proofs" of a point of view, is precisely that — a wrong use. With the caution that is due, and from among so many possibilities, we might look at the following quotation:

> "Everything God created is good; nothing is to be rejected when it is received with thanksgiving, for it is made holy by God's word and by prayer" (1 Tm 4:4-5).

Admittedly, the sacred author is addressing a particular problem; typical of the rhetoric used in a debate, we see references to "deceitful spirits" and "seared consciences." The "plausible liars" of which our author is speaking have been urging an "abstinence" from certain "foods," thereby disturbing some members of the community. Our author holds that such "foods" were "created to be received with thanksgiving," adding, "by believers who know the truth" (implying that his opponents are advocating a lie). Within the context of that debate (1 Tm 4:1-3) our quotation is given.

Created goods (such as foods) are to be "received." The fact that members of the community offer a "prayer" of "thanksgiving" (they "say grace," as we would put it) which borrows from the scriptures, or "word of God," is proof of that. Grace before meals becomes a "sacramental" of a larger approach to things, and that approach can be applied to the Church's use of "everything that is good."

Like the "prayer" offered when food is eaten, the Church's prayers in the celebration of sacramentals have been formed and informed by the "word of God."

In *form*, those prayers followed the traditional Jewish formularies, in which God is declared "blessed." A thanksgiving is offered to God for the good things he has made or accomplished. As such, the prayers used for sacramentals do resemble the sacraments, particularly the Eucharistic Prayers with their Prefaces that declare "it is right to give thanks."

In *content*, those prayers almost always refer to the scriptures, and borrow its wording. The prayer for the blessing of water, for example, naturally mentions the Baptism of Christ in the Jordan, but also recalls the creation of the waters at the beginning, the flood in Noah's day, and the crossing of the Red Sea.

In the light of what 1 Timothy has to say, and in the light of Vatican II's approach to word and world, we can arrive at something of a definition:

Sacramentals are: the goods of creation
which the Church receives
with thanksgiving
made holy by God's word and by prayer,
and which, like the sacraments they resemble,
proclaim to the world
the grace of Redemption
which transforms the world.

The debate about the number and nature of sacramentals, or how they resemble sacraments, is left to the theologians, for theirs is a living science. Vatican II, it must be remembered, stands at the beginning of an age as much as it marks the close of an era that is past; its statements sum up past development of doctrine, and provide a sound basis for continuing development.

But liturgy is a living science as well, and a lived experience. Signs of a redeemed creation can never have their say unless they are allowed to speak. A call for revision of rites is nothing less than this, an allowance to let things speak for themselves. Simple reverence for creation would call for this, and one hopes that this truth lies behind the mandate for reform.

AFTER VATICAN II

In calling for a revision of the rites (and sacramentals) of the Church, the *Constitution on the Sacred Liturgy* asks for the following:

— "a noble simplicity," one that makes the rites clear and devoid of needless repetition (Art 34);

— "a sense of community," one that is marked by the upbuilding of the complete Church-community (Art 42);

— "intelligent and active participation" (Art 79);

— "an intimate connection between rites and words"(Art 35);

— "new sacramentals," as need arises, or adaptation to various cultures requires (Art 79);

— "qualified lay persons"to administer certain sacramentals Art 79).

The requirements for revision, however, can lend themselves to our appreciation and understanding of sacramentals. Our acceptance (in every sense of that word) of redeemed creation may well be enhanced by looking at these guidelines more fully, as the Church continues into that age which began with the Vatican Council.

1. There should be an intimate connection between rite and Word.

When words and deeds combine, they should speak to each other; the rites should be marked by the intimacy of the dialogue, and the words should convey what is truly taking place. But that is part of the larger dialogue between Word and Deed. The "Word was made flesh," and the basic fact of Incarnation is not without its parallel in sacraments and sacramentals. God "said," and creation came to be, and when all had been completed, God "looked" and saw that it was "very good."

The revelation of the Word of God is precisely that — a revealing. As Eucharist takes place after the "Service of the Word," so should every other rite. The priority of the scriptures must be accepted as a lived truth. When the scriptures are read, proclaimed, or heard, a past is not being recalled; it is being relived. It addresses our human experiences and emotions, confirms them, and enables us to understand that the word of God is "living." The "two-edged sword" cuts between us and our understanding of the world.

In a word, no celebration should ever take place in the Church that does not center upon the Word.

2. There should be an intimate connection between rite and world.

We may pray to the Father who is "in heaven," but we ask that his will "be done on earth." There are not two worlds, or two cities (to borrow Augustine's own words), but one. If the poet was right when he said that no person "is an island," then the Church cannot be conceived as such. If anything, we are called to be servants of the world; God "so loved the world" that he sent Son to be servant. *Gaudium et Spes* had the courage to admit "the duty imposed on us to build up a better world," not a different one from that in which we live (Art 55).

There may have been times when one who entered the service of the Church was perceived to have left the world.

Shunning evil is not the same as shunning earth; "leaven" and "salt" never achieve their purpose if kept in containers.

Sacred rites, like Plato's child, "grow wings" as values are perceived, but that which is valuable first *is*. *A rite* is intended to help us perceive the world *aright*, among other purposes. We enter church, and depart through the same doors, and the world we enter upon leaving should be enhanced in our perception by that portion of the world we have just left.

3. The "noble simplicity" present in the world must be allowed to have its say.

Signs cannot be "sacred" unless they are truly signs in the first place, which means that they must be authentic. If someone unfamiliar with "holy water" should see it, that person perceives at least that it is water. A few drops at Baptism is not perceived as a cleansing flood, or a bath in which one is immersed. Oil that is immediately wiped off is not an anointing; oil that flows is, even if it tickles as it trickles. And cloth hidden by symbols is not perceived to be cloth, any more than a purificator is a robe. When one hears "Receive this white garment," and one sees a modified apron, more than the imagination is being stretched; truth is.

Water flows, oil oozes, vessels contain and clothing drapes. Space is not space if one cannot move about, and time is not time if it is not actually spent, used correctly instead of simply being used up, or merely "occupied." Any diminished "sign" diminishes the real, and what results is more a murmur than a word, neither "intelligent" nor "active."

4. A sense of community comes only from community.

On Harford Road in Baltimore, Md., there is one of those sign-boards in front of a church, and it really deserves to be called that, a "sign" board. The times of services, and the sermon topic are listed, and it's always interesting to see what's going to be said. At the heading, however, the name of the Pastor is given, and below his name this line appears: "Ministers — every member."

Certain sacramentals, the conciliar document states, are to be administered by "qualified lay persons." That has happened in the revision of the sacraments, to some degree. In the rites for the baptism of children, parents and godparents have been "given" a more prominent role, as have the sponsors in ceremonies for adult baptism. (One can legitimately ask if such persons have been "given" enough of a role, or whether the entire community present can think of itself as more than onlookers.) In the celebration of Holy Eucharist, in the services of Word and Sacrament, lay persons have assumed roles unthinkable in times past.

As for sacramentals, however, deeper questions must be asked and answered.

An obvious outcome, as regard these rites, is their celebration as communal events. So many "blessings" take place in privacy, with the presupposition that the Church is "spiritually" present; this is just another way of saying that nobody else is there except the priest. This is at best a deprivation, and an impoverishment; it is an irrational rationalization.

The Church has a right to its self-identity, and every effort to have the community experience itself in its entirety is to be applauded. Ordinations, or rites of religious profession, have meaning for specific groups (family, religious family), but there is a wider significance for the entire group. Weddings and funerals are important moments in the lives of individuals and individual families, but they are no less momentous for the community itself.

But more is involved than the mere assurance that at least a representative portion of the community is at hand. A theology of ministry is still unfolding, and while ministry is seen to begin with communal and liturgical recognition, the distinction between baptismal and ordained ministries is less than satisfactory.

For some sacramentals, such as the blessing of a home, the setting cannot be the local assembly. For such sacramentals, one may ask:

Who should "perform" the blessing of a home?

Who should bless things used in a home?

Who should bless the members of a family?

What role can be performed by those who "co-create" the elements of worship, or the buildings where worship takes place?

Who will call down God's blessing upon the blessed creation used by laborers and artists and ordinary folk?

The questions seem endless, but are actually one question: Who ministers?

To build a sense of community does not mean that the designated ministers must step aside, for the denigration of values lessens community, and that is a dangerous risk. In the realm of sacramentals, however, the answers to so many questions affect the entire people of God; solutions will effect community, hopefully, as what we do declares who we are.

In this regard, sacramentals can be seen as:

signs that *recall* the way in which ministries emerged, and *call* us to be a holy people;

signs that *declare* we are community;

signs that *oblige* us to build community; and,

signs that *foresee* — the future.

5. *New sacramentals are called for by the Church.*

The world changes, and we change with it. Today's mystery becomes tomorrow's discovery, but there are tomorrows that still call for discovery, and all the elements of our world are not yet categorized, filed, and otherwise consigned to lists of what is known or supposed.

Some symbols keep their mystery, like fire and candles, which we still light for special occasions and guests (even while the overhead lights are on), and everyone can see without a need for candles; we still need the fascination they provide. Certain symbols will have to be seen again, made new, for too many they have ceased to speak; but they retain their value in another way, like incense, which speaks to us from its use in scriptures if not from the world of everyday.

And some signs will have to be discovered. Liturgy is a

living tradition, and needs and occasions will arise that call for celebration of their sacredness. The moments of our lives cry out for some attention that provides them meaning. Our society changes at a rapid pace, and care must be taken lest certain rites of our passage, our pilgrimage, are passed over without being received with a thankfulness made holy by God's word and prayer.

In the revised ceremonies for the baptism of children, for example, a collect is provided that mentions adoption. What of a child, already baptized, who is adopted? Does the need exist for parents and community to celebrate the specialness of this gift? Are we not all "adopted" daughters and sons?

Things new, and new relationships; moments special to some, that speak to all; emerging ministries — these and more await liturgical discovery, and an openness to the world will see "new" sacramentals emerge.

PART TWO

THE SACREDNESS OF TIME

Our lives are marked by the passing of time, and we change as the seasons do. The revelation of God to his chosen took place through events observable in history, and was fully made in the person of Jesus Christ who "progressed steadily in wisdom and age and grace" (Lk 2:52).

The Church, which is his fullness, moved steadily from age to age, reliving the events that gave her birth, and renewing herself by celebration of the Paschal Mystery, so that "*day by day* the Lord added to the number of those who were being saved" (Acts 2:47).

The yearly celebration of Easter became the center of an expansion that moved outward to become a liturgical year. In individual localities, the memory of those who died for their faith began to be recalled, and their "memorials" celebrated each year. The great events of Christ's life became the focus of yearly celebrations, just as Judaism kept its festivals to mark the changing points of the passing months. Together with Easter, and Sunday as the Lord's Day, a weekly Easter as it was viewed, the Church celebrates those who had risen with him to new and glorious life.

As all our days are marked by work and leisure, the Church's day was marked by prayer, and certain hours of the day lent themselves more readily to public worship.

Israel's Psalms became the Church's hymns, and were arranged to be prayerfully sung as the hours of the day passed.

If one can view God's "Blessing" of the seventh day as the first "sacramental" within sacred history, the Church was seen as "blessing" every day of the year with his praises. Time itself was seen as holy, and sanctified as the followers of Christ took time to ponder the timeless that was in their midst. Theirs was the view of Ecclesiastes:

> "He has made everything appropriate to its time, and has put the timeless into their hearts. . . . What now is has already been; what is to be, already is; and God restores what would otherwise be displaced" (Ecc 3:11,15).

Within the Catholic tradition, the days of the week are more than mere echo of the first days of creation. God is seen as still moving through his creation as when Eden was fresh with first and new life. Tennessee Williams summed up our approach to the sacredness of time: "The day turns holy as God moves through it."

CHAPTER IV

THE LITURGICAL YEAR

The Church believes that it is her duty, and her privilege, "to celebrate the saving work" of Christ. She does so "in a sacred commemoration on certain days throughout the course of the year. Once each week, on the day which she has called the Lord's Day, she keeps the memory of the Lord's Resurrection. She also celebrates it, once every year, together with his blessed passion, at Easter, that most solemn of all feasts.

"In the course of the year, moreover, she unfolds the whole mystery of Christ from the incarnation and nativity to the ascension, to Pentecost and the expectation of the blessed hope of the coming of the Lord" (Const. on Sacred Liturgy, Art 102).

The year, known as the "liturgical year," must be considered as a sacramental. Time itself is drawn into the redemptive work of Christ which took place at a moment in time, and which continues until time is no more. With Christ, the Church relives the events that marked his appearance among us, conditioned as it was by the elements of time and season, of festival and fast. Yearly she celebrates what is most important, just as each of us takes time for what we consider important.

When Luke set out to open his Gospel, he could state that his purpose was to construct "the whole sequence of events from the beginning" (Lk 1:2), and asserted that this was "carefully traced." As the Church's observance of those events, according to days and seasons, began to take shape, there was no such construction. As with time itself, things just happened. We can trace an intricate pattern, or series of patterns, to the liturgical year, but only from our point in time, looking back at a development that took centuries.

The Week

The Church, formed within the matrix of Judaism, with its weekly observance of Sabbath, as well as its yearly festivals commemorative of God's interventions in her behalf, readily accommodated itself to marking sacred time in terms of the week. The account of creation in seven days, and the blessing of "the seventh day," was already a "sacramental" to the followers of Jesus. Two factors would combine to see "the first day of the week," so symbolic of new creation and so descriptive of the moment when Christ rose from the dead, move the Church from observance of Sabbath to the specific celebration of Sunday as "the Lord's Day" (a term already in use as the New Testament was being written, as found in Rev 1:10). .

The first, of course, would be the gospels' accounts of the Resurrection. The second, restored by the "vigil Masses" on Saturday as part of Sunday's observance, springs directly from Jewish observance. Keeping to the customary observance, Jewish Christians would refrain from walking long distances on the Sabbath. They would meet once that restriction had ended at sundown, which was already, by Jewish reckoning, the first day of the week. When the Church finally left the environments of Judaism, Sunday became the day of weekly observance.

By the second century of the Christian era, Justin the Martyr could observe that Christians "gather together on Sunday not only because this first day is that on which the Lord God ... created the world, but also because Jesus our

Savior rose from the dead on the same day (*Apologia* I, 67). Sunday consequently forms a weekly celebration of the Resurrection of Christ, and does so long before any yearly observance. If the Sabbath was joyfully welcomed, as it continues to be in the Jewish Prayerbook, Sunday was received with no less a sense of welcome and joy. Even as penitential practices became prominent, and at times seemed to overshadow any sense of celebration, Sundays retained their festive character.

A Yearly Sunday

From the dawn of Christian worship, Sunday remained the principal celebration of the Easter event. As such, the year is marked by the passing of Sundays more than by the passing of entire weeks. "Evening came, and morning followed," Genesis states, as day follows day in creation's story (Gn 1:5), and for Sundays, evenings, completed by mornings, marked the time for celebration of the Eucharist.

The Exodus had taken place at night, and Christian associations with nighttime (Christ arose "while it was still dark," according to Jn 20:1, and followers were bidden to wait for his glorious appearance "whether at dusk, at midnight, when the cock crow, or at early dawn," according to Mk 13:35) led to a "night-watch," or vigil. This became the principal observance of Easter, associated with the Jewish feast of Passover.

The intimate connection between risen life and one's participation in new life through Baptism exerted its influence upon the Pachal Solemnity. The Church kept vigil together with her catechumens, and Easter night became the principal (if not sole) occasion for the "Easter Sacrament." Like a stone that forms ripples when cast into a pond, the celebration of Easter expanded from its own evening-and-morning to the days that preceded and came afterward, and it is the sacrament of Baptism that exerted the strongest influence upon this development of many days in which to celebrate a single event.

The witness of the earliest centuries mentions a period of

fasting for at least a few days before the conferral of Baptism. In the 3rd century, Hippolytus mentions Friday and Satuday as days on which "those to be enlightened fasted and prayed." The same century saw the expansion of that preparatory period into a complete week. At this point in history, we are but a short step away from the development of "Holy Week," and a complete commemoration of events that began with the Lord's triumphal entry into his own city.

By the end of that century, the period of fasting had grown to six weeks, or about forty days. Sundays still retained their festive character, but the season of Lent had taken its development, and the forty days (symbolic of the forty years of Israel's wanderings in the desert, and the Lord's own fast of forty days) became a fixed period of time. Finally, in the 7th century, with the curious need for precision it was felt that the complete number of days for fasting should be observed, and the Wednesday before the First Sunday of Lent came to be regarded as a starting point.

There was a host of influences at work, not least among them the preparation of the candidates for Baptism. The ceremonies attending this preparation became defined and set days were fixed for each. Their names were "enrolled," and they were "given" the teaching of Apostles (Creed), the Lord's Prayer, and the Gospels; each "tradition" was appointed to a specific Sunday in Lent.

The period after the yearly observance of Easter also witnessed a similar expansion. The concept of a complete week, so that a sense of "beginning" could be recaptured "on the eighth day," brought about the extension of Easter Sunday into the days that followed. Judaism had observed what we call an "octave," and the Jewish feast of Pentecost lent itelf to the concept of Easter as "a festival of fifty days," an idea that has been restored in the renewal of the Church's liturgy as mandated by Vatican II.

Luke's manner of describing the descent of the Holy Spirit "when the day of Pentecost came" (Acts 2:1), together with his reference to "the course of forty days" (Acts 1:3) in which the Risen One appeared to his disciples and spoke with them, greatly influenced this expansion. The relationship between Easter and Pentecost was not without its reference to the candidates for Baptism. Those not baptized on Easter night were presented at the night-watch for Pentecost, and were baptized then.

With that delightful sense of the "genuinely human" that finds its "echoes" within the Church, the newly baptized lay aside their "white garments," bestowed during their baptism, on the Sunday after Easter. (Traditionally, this has been given the name "Low Sunday," for the "low" which the newly baptized experienced, after the "high point" of their lives came to its liturgical climax during the Easter week.

Time progressed, and as the Church settled down in the world, and made itself "at home," so to speak, Easter (now a season with "before" and "after") took on a new dimension. Over the course of centuries, as the Church grew in number, the emphasis upon Baptism began to diminish. At first, the remainder of the community entered into a spirit of prayer and fasting together with, and on behalf of, the catechumens; as their number decreased, more and more attention was paid to Lent as a period of prayer and fasting. With the growth in understanding of the sacrament of Reconciliation, the penitential nature of Lent, at first confined to the penitents preparing for that sacrament, was extended to all members of the Church, and Lent (as we have come to know it) slowly began to lose its intimate connection with Easter, a process that was not without gain and loss at the same time.

A Second Cycle

The development of the liturgical year took centuries to reach any completion (if indeed we can speak of it as completed at all, without any growth in years to come). At first, as in the development of Easter, the celebrations of the Church were exclusively lived experiences of the redemptive work of Christ. With the passing of time, Easter began to be separated into components, and attention paid to each incident that marked the saving event.

Thus, Friday before Easter, which in the early days was

marked by no particular observance, came to be known as Godly (Good) Friday. A liturgy slowly developed around the reading (or chanting) of the Passion, and, in time, around the "veneration" of the cross. The Lord's Supper became the central focus for the preceding Thursday, now prefixed by the word "holy." The observance of the entire week, an observance intimately connected with the city of Jerusalem itself, reached into other parts of the world where the Church's liturgy was developing.

With the passing of time, however, other aspects of the life of Christ gave rise to considerable reflection and thought, and eventually to the celebration of those events. It is a process not unlike that in which the Gospels took shape. Mark (considered the earliest Gospel) makes no mention of the birth or childhood of Jesus, a situation which is reme- died by accounts of his infancy in Matthew and Luke. Heresies that called the Incarnation into doubt had their roles to play as well.

And so we see "a second cycle" of celebrations begin to emerge towards the end of the second century. By the mid- dle of the 4th century Christmas is listed in the calendar of the Church at Rome. In the East, Epiphany was the central celebration, recalling the Incarnation of Christ together with his Baptism by John (possibly an attempt to transfer the baptismal significance of Easter to this feast). Both were celebrated in Rome by the end of the 4th century, and the stage is set for "a second cyle," patterned after that which grew up around the celebration of Easter.

Christmas received its expansion in the form of Advent, to prepare for it, and Epiphany, to bring the cycle to its close. The process resembles the development of Easter, but not completely, for while Advent now seems to be a prepa- ration for Christmas, it was originally a season to introduce the entire year.

In modern society, at least in Western culture, the "new year" is taken to begin on January 1st, but this was not always so, nor is it so for other cultures, or for the religious calendar of Judaism. The concept of "new year" moved about like a celebration looking for a date to be observed;

some of the traces of "new year" on April 1st, as it was observed in France centuries ago, still linger on in the festive pranks of "April's fool-day," now termed "April Fools' Day." Spring was a good time to start a year, and April 1st as good a day as any.

Originally, the beginning of the Church's year appears to have been observed on March 25th, which was seen not only as the day on which the "Word became flesh," but as the actual day on which the world was created. "In the beginning," as a phrase that opens both Genesis and the Gospel of John, was taken to mark the beginning of the liturgical year.

With the celebration of the Lord's Nativity, however, a change began to occur, and the time around Christmas was understood as appropriate to mark the opening of the liturgical year. As it took shape in fourth century Spain, from which it moved to France and Italy, Advent (from *adventus*, or "coming") was conceived as a time of preparation for the final appearance of Christ at end-time. Within the span of mere decades, it began to be seen as a time of preparation for Christmas as well. Both elements merge in our present-day celebrations, but the element of expectation for final glory is uppermost, even if not acknowledged by commercial interests.

Thus Christmas received its season of preparation, and like the season of Lent, Advent was marked by purple, and something of a penitential character was given to it. As a season, it is one of the richest times within the liturgical year. To a degree, it can be said to sum up the entire year; it points out the sacredness of time itself, which awaits its completion in the timelessness of a kingdom yet to come.

From earliest times, Christmas was followed by the observance of the feasts of saints which follow in their order. The feast of St. Stephen, it seems, was observed as early as the 4th century (at least in the East), placing it at a date earlier than the observance of Christmas itself. The other feasts that followed (Holy Innocents, St. John the Evangelist) only served to form something of an "octave" of Christmas. It is a development that would have happened anyway, given the similarity of this cycle to that of Easter.

Following the feast of the Nativity and its Octave we find a celebration that predates Christmas. Epiphany (a word that means "manifestation" or "appearance") appears to be connected with a pagan feast that occurred on January 6th. That day was marked by a festival that celebrated the "birth" of light, as the longer hours of actual daylight were noticed, and dark winter began to draw to its close. Popular belief held that water was changed to wine, symbolic of the approach of spring and nature's transformation. For Christians, this pagan feast soon became the festival of the birth of him who is the Light of the world, and the wedding feast of Cana naturally suggested itself; the Baptism of Christ, when his "light" was seen to have manifested itself publicly, was also incorporated into the celebration of Epiphany. In the West, emphasis was placed upon the "appearance" of the Magi, and so the revelation of Christ to the Gentiles became the dominant theme.

With the development of this period after Christmas a 4th century celebration, now called the Feast of the Presentation of the Lord, was eventually added. It was a little "epiphany," when Christ's "appearance" at the temple was recalled, together with Simeon's declaration that he was a "light of revelation to the Gentiles" (Lk 2:32). That event, recorded by Luke (2:22-38), became the occasion for the blessing of lights, or candles, and became popularly known as "Candlemas Day." It served to bring this "second cycle" to its close, in much the same way that Pentecost completed the celebration of Easter.

Later Development

From a rather simple arrangement, the liturgical year grew like topsy. One area borrowed a celebration from another, and *vice versa*, and missionaries carried with them the celebrations of their own church, until it could be asked if there were a single day that wasn't special. Into the yearly cycle which at first commemorated only the events of our redemption, and later all the significant events in the life of

Christ, a complete cycle devoted to the saints, and to the Virgin Mary in particular, was added. The "Sanctoral Cycle" and the "Marian Cycle" became entirely separate in time. Although the Marian celebrations would be the last to be added to the calendar, by the time the liturgical year reached it completion, those observances formed a complete cycle in and of themselves. In its structure, it paralleled the Christ cycle, beginning with conception and birth, and closing with death, rising and glorification.

As for the Sanctoral Cycle, its growth developed in a perfectly natural way. The first saints to receive attention were the martyrs, those members of the community who suffered death for their faith. They became heroes to the remainder of the community, and the days of their martyrdom were observed by their communities as "birthdays into eternal life." All burials were occasions for festivity, unmarred by any notion of mourning or grief. Our memories being what they are, the anniversaries of their death were recalled quite naturally within the celebration of the Eucharist. The accounts of their deaths were recorded and preserved, and read to the gathered assembly. The concept of their power to intercede on behalf of their communities was a natural outflowing of the belief in the "communion of saints," and some of the earliest prayers for their "feasts" referred to this quite unashamedly. Oftentimes their tombs were marked with inscriptions to which the phrase "pray for us" was added.

By the end of the 6th century, as the calendar of a particular church was "adopted" by another community, the feasts of martyrs were also borrowed, and the accounts of their deaths were written down to provide models of behavior and exhortations to similar faithfulness. The end result was the multiplication of such observances, and soon other saintly women and men were to be remembered as well. It was not long before a choice had to be made as to which saint would be celebrated on a particular day.

For many of us, especially at house-cleaning time, less is more. That was never true with the calendar. Since the time of the Reformation efforts have been made to restrict the number of saint's days, and the Second Vatican Council, in its reform of the calendar, set about to do this with some degree of success. Yet heroic sanctity needs to be celebrated, and women and men, whose lives and deeds serve to inspire our own, continue to rise to the fore in the Church's life, and so the addition of their observances will continue to fill the calendar, and to thwart any attempt to restrict the number of celebrations.

One other development of the liturgical calendar needs to be mentioned, and that is the observance of special days that honor a dogma. Trinity Sunday, the Solemnity of Corpus Christi, or the Sunday devoted to the Holy Family, to name but a few, began to be inserted into the calendar. Eventually the full flowering of Easter's celebration would lend itself to days such as these, so that an octave became a part of the celebration. It was not long before such octaves overlapped, and even the experts in liturgical matters needed an ecclesiastical slide-rule to determine the calendar for each year. The simplification of the calendar by the Second Vatican Council put an end to this intricate arrangement. However we may view such a development, it does serve to point out how "special" days and seasons actually are, and how practicality is often lost in the need to celebrate the triumphs of grace and the awesomeness of great truths.

As with other sacramentals, seasons and special days are *signs that remember* a truth or a moment; *signs that declare* time to be sacred; *signs that oblige* us to recall a mystery, or exhibit a virtue, and some days are known as "holydays of obligation" (a term that tends to lessen the deeper sense of obligation one must have); and *signs that foresee* the day when we shall behold the mysteries we ponder and the glory bestowed upon our sisters and brothers in the Lord.

The *Constitution on the Sacred Liturgy* would have the cycle of our redemption restored to its primacy, and the seasons of redemption regain their original purpose and character. This is especially true, for example, with the observance of Lent; its connection with the RCIA has restored this "penitential" season to its original status as a period of preparation for baptism, and a time for the community to ready itself for the renewal of baptismal commitment. Only those saints have been retained whose celebration has a truly universal significance. Individual nations and areas may choose to include the observances that are special in their own life and culture. There is much to guide the future in the principals of the calendar's reform with which we are now familiar. The Easter and Christmas cycles stand out within the course of the year, and the later developments (Seasons after Epiphany and Pentecost) have disappeared. If the term "Ordinary Time" does not appeal to our imaginations, or adequately sum up the mystery of all time as sacred, it best describes what such intervening time actually represents — the mystery of holiness within all that is ordinary.

The number of "feastdays" for the saints has been reduced, and emphasis upon the Church's daily cycle of readings does allow the Christ-event to assume its rightful priority. There is a temptation to return to the recent past, and make the "memorials" of the saints the focus of the daily liturgy. It is a temptation that will be resisted, hopefully, for the thrust of the present reform has been to "insert" these memorials into the principal cycle, which is the continuing story of our salvation, the mystery of Jesus Christ, upon whom the saints focused their attention.

The mention of the saint of the day can take place within the Eucharistic Prayer, and their heroism can be recalled in the daily homily (which should never be omitted). It takes little imagination and effort to relate the life of a saint to the truths found in the scriptures selected for daily use; in fact, this is the very basis for added insight.

What remains for the years to come?

1. The basic thrust of the reforms mandated by Vatican II should be reinforced constantly, and not lessened or lost to sight.

This means that the restoration of Sunday to its primacy should not be lessened by having that day devoted to a cause, however noble, and however great the pressure from interested groups. "Vocation Sunday," or "Right-to-Life Sunday," for example, should never become terms for the weekly Easter. Those concepts can receive proper attention without lessening the Sunday observance; attaching such labels to the weekly Easter does little to enhance the necessary observance of the Risen One, and the obligation to recommit ourselves each week to the baptism whereby we rose with him.

The liturgy of each day should have its own say, and special observances of a saint should be precisely that — special. The patrons of dioceses or parish churches should be observed; saints proper to an area should be celebrated; but to make every day a festival only serves to lessen the very notion of what it means to be festive.

There is a further possibility for heightening our sense of each day as a celebration of Christ; it lies with those who oversee the development of liturgical practices for specific regions. Alternative prayers are provided for Sundays, but a lacuna does exist on the weekdays in ordinary time, when the orations from any ordinary Sunday may be used, with no guide to assist the celebrant. There is a need for orations on these weekdays, just as the seasons of Advent or Lent are marked by prayers for the days of the week. Compositions, based on the scriptural readings for those days, would be a welcome addition.

With the renewed interest in Holy Scripture, a further suggestion is made. Oftentimes the connection between the orations and the readings is completely missing. This is especially true now that we have a cycle of three years. One could hope that orations, drawing their language from the sacred texts, might be forthcoming for each Sunday in each of the three cycles, and that each of the readings would lend their wording to the principal orations. Nothing would prevent the composition of Prefaces for these Sundays, a factor that would serve to unite the Liturgies of Word and Sacrament.

2. Efforts to formulate an ecumenical calendar should continue to be encouraged at every level.

This is a serious undertaking, and one that is filled with promise. Something of its completion may take place on the local level, and not be confined to a yearly observance of the Week of Prayer for Christian Unity. Dates significant to other churches (particularly to communities located within the parish boundaries) can be observed in prayerfulness. The General Intercessions offer ample opportunity for this.

3. Our Jewish origins should be brought to the fore.

The celebrations of the Jewish calendar should also receive our prayerful recognition within the liturgy of the appropriate days. A special note of thankfulness, so essential to the very notion of Eucharist, and so formed by Paul's own on that subject, should be given to that people from whom we have received "adoption, the glory, . . . the worship and the promises . . . and the Messiah" (Rom 9:3-5). For all that we have received, a liturgical note could only echo Paul's own statement: "Blessed forever be God who is over all! Amen." (Rom 9:5).

One feels a natural reluctance to appropriate the celebrations of God's People as our own (Seder suppers and the like); but the events that mark the Jewish calendar form a part of our own history. Yet one can only sense a lack of completeness when the observances that Jesus and his disciples kept are allowed to pass unnoticed.

4. All that is genuinely human should be celebrated.

National "feasts" have been introduced into specific calendars, complete with readings and texts. But nothing prevents other days, whether of national or purely local importance, from being celebrated as well. This is especially so when one considers that the General Intercessions (the Prayer *of* the Faithful, as distinct from the Eucharistic Prayer as the "prayer *for* the faithful") represents the opportunity of the Church to enact her proper role as an intercessor before God on behalf of the peoples of the world.

And the achievements of individuals within the community deserve our attention within the liturgy. What brings joy to one is best appreciated within the context of a worshiping community, which is the perfect setting for joys that are enhanced and shared.

CHAPTER V

THE HOURS OF THE DAY

In regarding time as sacred, with its seasons of grace, Catholic worship looks not only to the year, with its divisions into weeks, but at the day itself, with its divisions into hours. The liturgical year celebrates days, individually or in succession, as sacred times, but every day itself is made holy. We settle into patterns of daily behavior, with set times for work and meals and rest and leisure, and if there is anything that needs "blessing" it's the routine of every day.

The Liturgy of the Hours, which the Church borrowed from the daily devotions of her members, has been called the means whereby "the whole course of the day and night is made holy by the praise of God" (Const. on Sacred Liturgy, Art 84). If, in the very course of time, that worship was called "the divine office," and considered "a duty for the Church," the notion still persisted that "by offering these praises to God" the Church "stood before his throne" (Art 85).

It is regarded as a sacramental, and rightly so (even if not by all theologians), for it provides the very setting of Eucharistic worship each day; resembles it in its offering of thankful praise; and teaches that each day is sacred, even if not a festival, and special, even if not a feast. Perhaps it is this view which led to the multiplication of feasts and observances; a truth was at work, even if the manner of expressing it was less than desirable, and resulted in hiding the sacredness of "ordinary time" from sight.

Anchored in A History

The foundations upon which the Liturgy of the Hours rests can be said to lie amid the rubble of a devastated Jerusalem. When the Holy City was destroyed in the 6th century before Christ, and God's people found themselves exiles in a foreign land, they were distant not only from their homes but from all that had sustained them as a people. Without the temple and its rituals, and without the sustenance that their liturgies had provided them, a new form of worship was to emerge.

That era is considered the time when the synagogue-service took its shape. There, "by the streams of Babylon," they "remembered Zion" (Ps 137:1). It seemed that remembrance was all that was left to them, as is the nature with memories. They "came together" (a phrase that translated into the word *synagogue*), and their shared memories took the form of recalling all that God had done for them in times past.

Whether they gathered primarily for worship is not clear; the purpose may have been instructional, or simply to regain a sense of identity. But worship it did become. The retelling of the past came in the form of what we know as "readings." If their "captors" had asked of them "the lyrics" to their songs (Ps 137:4), they preserved their songs to complement the readings. Readings and Psalms were followed by words of instruction, and finally by prayers which "blessed" God for past interventions, and invoked his continued assistance.

Without temple or priesthood, without furnishings or sacrifices, the laity gathered and created a form of worship that has survived to the present. The temple would be rebuilt, and finally destroyed again in 70 A.D., but the synagogue-service would survive. When Jesus "came to

Nazareth," he entered the synagogue "as he was in the habit of doing," and "stood up to do the reading." Then, "rolling up the scroll, he handed it back to the assistant, and sat down" (Lk 4:16,20).

We naturally do things in patterns, and assume postures for specific tasks. The synagogue-service, although a liturgy of words, was a liturgy of sitting and standing, and ministries were involved. If "all in the synagogue had their eyes fixed on him" (Lk 4:20), it is because they were accustomed to give their attention to the speaker, and not simply because he was who he was.

Times for Prayer

If the pattern of the synagogue-service would lend itself to the Liturgy of the Hours (as to the Liturgy of the Word at Mass), so too was the custom of praying at specific hours to have its impact as well. When Peter and John went "up to the temple for prayer at the three o'clock (ninth) hour" (Acts 3:1), the presumption is that this was a time set aside for prayer. The manual of Discipline discovered among the Dead Sea scrolls records set times. The community prayed "at the beginning of light's mastery," and again "at the highest point of its course," as well as at the close of day "when light withdrew to its appointed place." It is not unlike the prophet Daniel who "continued his custom of going home to kneel in prayer and give thanks to his God in the upper chamber three times a day, with the windows open toward Jerusalem" (Dn 6:11). As early as the 2nd century, Christians were enouraged to say the Lord's Prayer three times a day.

The natural "hinges" of the day, morning and evening, would be natural moments to turn to God in prayer, as they still are for Jew and Christian alike. Those two times would become the pivotal points of the Liturgy of the Hours as well. The other hours of the day, set aside for prayer, would also come into play. Past examples would be recalled, and the custom of "three times a day" would see the third, sixth and ninth hours referred to as "apostolic." The "third hour" had marked the descent of the Spirit at Pentecost (Acts 2:15), the "sixth hour" that time when Peter prayed atop a roof (Acts 10:9), as well as "the ninth hour," or "three o'clock," when Peter and John went up to the temple (Acts 3:1).

Those hours represented the normal divisions of the Roman day, and the ordinary was given special meaning in the light of what the Word of God had to say. At first, since the Church had not yet gained the freedom to worship publicly, those special times were the customary hours for private prayer. Perhaps they were thought of as bridging a distance, for while all were not together as community, a common practice gave assurance that all were together in the presence of God. Christ's injunction to pray "in private," in their rooms with doors closed (Mt 7:6), did not prevent his followers from realizing that they were one in him.

Although set times were never the same in every time or place, nor decreed with any precision, private prayer was soon to become official worship done in public. When churches could be built, or basilicas created in the larger city (or simply "taken over" and existing buildings made "sacred"), purely private devotions became liturgies, built upon the pattern of readings, psalms and prayers, together with some type of instruction at times.

Most likely out of purely practical concerns, the morning and evening hours became the most important. By the end of the 4th century, we find St. Ambrose urging the faithful of Milan to take part in the prayers at morning and evening. As the workday followed its course, the other hours for prayer were left to the bishops and their clergy. It was their "duty" to be present, and most likely others joined in to embody the whole Church at prayer, but it hardly seems likely that they were able to do so, or even encouraged to take their part.

A Divine Duty

By the time that Ambrose could encourage attendance at the *morning praise* and *evening praise* (which soon became titles for these "hours" of prayer), another development happened to fix the arrangement of the divine office. That was the rise of monasticism, which began in the 3rd century. Perhaps it was the end of the age of martyrs that led to this, with the truly difficult becoming a substitute for martyrdom, an effort to resemble Christ by "dying to self" if not by actually dying. Women and men went into the desert to pray, and communities were formed, in which prayer was done in common.

A life of prayer could now be cultivated, and the Book of Psalms began to be truly appreciated as prayers sung, and sung in common. Psalmody was to become, thereby, the principal element in the Liturgy of the Hours.

Not all of these communities would remain in the desert for long, however. With the building of public places for worship, religious communities offered a valuable resource for the Liturgy of the Hours then taking shape. Monasteries came to be built within the cities, and close to the basilicas, and by the 6th century this was more the norm than the exception. In smaller churches, Lauds and Vespers (designations for the morning and evening "hours" respectively) were observed, but in the cathedral churches, the complete round of daily worship could be accomplished. Paul's injunction to "pray without ceasing" finally must have appeared to reach a fulfillment that would have done him proud.

THE INDIVIDUAL HOURS

Morning Praise and Evening Praise.

The oldest parts of the Liturgy of the Hours to become proper "hours" were the praises offered at morning and evening.

The first came to be called *laudes matutinae,* literally "praises at morning-star," and was simply called *Lauds,* a word that speaks for itself. Its major element is the psalmody, and the *Apostolic Constitutions,* which reveals the liturgy in Antioch at the close of the 4th century, directed that certain psalms appropriate to the morning hours should be sung. (One of them, Psalm 62, begins its address to God as "my God whom I seek," which in some versions read, "whom I seek at break of day") In time, the Canticle of Zachary came to represent the highpoint of this hour, because of its mention of "the Dayspring" that would "shine on those who sit in darkness" (Lk 1:78,79).

The second major "hour," popularly known as Vespers for so long (from the Latin *vespera*, or evening-star), resembles the morning praises, with its psalms, reading and prayers. In time, the Canticle of Mary, which praises God "who has done great things for me" (Lk 1:49) became its crowning point; not merely because it summed up the day, as many took it to mean, but because it summed up God's "mercy from age to age" (Lk 1:50). The praise of God was always for all the saving works performed since creation itself. Private prayer may have given rise to the official prayer of the Church, but public worship is always that — a public and communal proclamation of the mighty deeds of God.

An earlier name for this hour was *lucernarium*, the "lighting of the lamps," a basic activity at nightfall. For those familiar with Jewish practice, the lighting of lamps in church was but a continuation of what took place at home. To this day, as sundown takes place, and Sabbath begins, the mother of the home "blesses" the Sabbath lights, as she "blesses" God for his gift of light.

Midday Hours.

The third, sixth and ninth hours were also marked by psalms (fewer in number), a short reading, and prayer. As monasticism developed, and hymns were added to start each hour of prayer, these "midday hours" (as they are now called) became fixed, and attached to centering upon the time of day they were celebrated. Morning praise and evening praise, as principal hours, came to reflect the season of the year, or special feast, while the midday hours kept their daily significance. For years, interestingly enough, they concluded with the simple recitation of the Our Father, recalling the early suggestion that Christians should recite this prayer at least three times a day.

Night Office.

The monasteries gave rise to this hour, but it had its origins in the private prayers which Christians were accustomed, and encouraged, to pray. Midnight might seem an odd hour to rise for prayer, but the custom was observed. It seems to have been connected, by some, to the "midnight" appearance of "the groom" in the parable of the Ten Virgins (Mt 25:6), and found reinforcement in Acts, where Paul and Silas "were praying about midnight" (Acts 16:25).

In monasteries, this "hour" became the longest, and there was really no attempt to find psalms that could lend meaning to the nighttime hours. The liturgy for this hour of prayer seems to have followed the practice of the earliest days, when women and men formed monastic communities, and simply went through the psalter in numerical order. As this hour developed, it became something like the drawer that everyone has, in which things that have no place of their own are kept. Not only were there readings from scripture, but in time the writings of the Church Fathers, and ultimately the lives of the saints, found their way into *Matins* (so called because it led into the pre-dawn hours of the day).

Compline.

Finally, as things developed, another "hour" was added, again due to monastic life. Put quite simply, it was a prayer before retiring, the "Now I Lay Me Down To Sleep" of monks and nuns. For the longest time it was prayed not in church or chapel, but in the sleeping-quarters. Psalm 91 was the psalm recited, or sung, with its reference to God as the "refuge," who will "rescue" one from "the terror of the night."

As it entered the official liturgy, it did so with all the finishing touches, especially a final hymn to Mary. In its outlook, and even in its wording, this hour sought the same things of the traditional Child's Prayer; it asked to have God "keep" the sleeping soul, or receive it "if I should die before I wake."

To the Present

The history of the development of the Liturgy of the Hours would demand at least one book to treat it with any scope or purpose. That history, however, could be summed up in a single factor: what began as prayers privately recited by the Christian of whatever state, lay or cleric, and became public prayer for all, eventually became the official prayer recited by clergy alone. Whatever richness in hymns, antiphons and prayers, whether collects or litanies, the failure of the liturgy of the hours to enrich the lives of all the faithful is just too obvious a fact to allow one to declare otherwise. The use of Latin had a tremendous role to play in hiding these liturgical actions from the mainstream of the Church's life. It led to the development of "devotions," which tended to become a substitute for liturgy, and often paralleled the liturgy. The "Angelus," recited three times a day, became the popular form of the liturgy of the hours for most layfolk. However popular Millet's famous painting may be, and however touching, one is forced to admit that the Christian community had certainly allowed itself to dwindle down to the gospel's minimum of "two" who would be "gathered" in his name!

Even the *Constitution on the Sacred Liturgy* (Articles 83 to 101) could not break the logjam of an official prayer confined to only a portion of the entire Church. We might *say* that the liturgy of the hours is "the prayer of the whole Church," but the facts simply contradict such a statement. It is, and continues to be, an "office" which properly belongs to the clergy, and to religious women and men in their communal life. To be sure, there is value in knowing that someone is praying on behalf of the whole Church, and that this is taking place somewhere or other. But there is a lessening of values as well, and the loss, for all practical purposes, of a tradition that one feels must be preserved.

Even the popular name for the liturgy of the hours contains an irony. The term "breviary" belies its actual meaning, when referring to the book(s) that must be used. Large books were required in the days before printing was invented, simply to allow the entire group of cantors to read the music together. Consequently a small piece of paper was drawn up to provide a simple outline of the books, indicating which book, or which location within a book, was to be used on a particular day. For such a purpose a single piece of paper was all that was needed, and because it was so *brief*, it was called "brief" (*breviarium*, in Latin). That piece of paper grew to become four volumes, and even with the reforms of Vatican II, four volumes it remains!

A Pastoral Solution

1. Those whose duty it is to pray the liturgy of the hours should make every effort to do so in common, especially the principal hours at morning and eventide.

Until a true revision takes place, one in which the treasure of the Church's daily prayer is restored to the entire Church, those who are "bound" to its recitation can lead the effort (a suggestion already made in the General Instruction to the Liturgy of the Hours, Arts. 20 and 21). The question remaining is a purely practical one, namely that of books or booklets; supply and demand are forces that exert an influence in liturgical matters as much as they do in the field of economics.

Parishes can establish the patterns for such "hours," and if the churches or chapels aren't filled to capacity, at least the entire community will know that a truly representative portion of the Church is offering prayers on behalf of all. This will allow a communion of mind and intent, even if all cannot pray at the same time and in the same place.

2. The official "hours" can become the normal means for public devotions, and the start of meetings and such.

Once again the principal difficulty is the supply of materials, and once again the law of demand-and-supply will have to come to the fore. The possibilities, however, are endless. Novenas and popular devotions continue in use, but without the richness inherent in the hours of the Church's prayer. The intercessions at these hours could easily be adapted to whatever devotions draw a number of the faithful. In particular, the Christian "wake-services" could assume the pattern of the hour in question, especially the evening hour.

The establishment of some form of daily prayer apart from the Mass could well serve to become the proper means of celebrating the saint of the day. A reading from Scripture, together with the account of that saint's life or martyrdom, would keep the memorial of the saints in the forefront of the community's celebration. Followed by intercessions, especially any prayers composed by that saint, or important in her or his life (such as "The Breastplate of St. Patrick"), such a pattern would truly serve as a complement to the Eucharist, and allow the primacy of the Christ-event to be observed within the Mass.

3. *One's own devotions can reflect the liturgical hours.*

The principal difficulty has been the failure of the revision of the liturgy of the hours to become truly the prayer of the entire people. No one doubts the real need that is felt for some form of prayer to render the day sacred, and to heighten a sense of praying in common with the entire Church.

A temporary solution would be the development of a course of daily bible readings and prayers. There has been a continued and growing interest in reading and praying the Bible, especially one suited to Catholic usage, and to the entire liturgical year, with its seasons and solemn days. Many undertake to read the Bible, beginning with Genesis, only to find that Genesis also marks the end of such an attempt, or Exodus, for those more adventurous and persistent.

A real need exists to develop an approach to Bible reading that is attuned to the liturgical year, and which spurs a prayerfulness which marks the liturgy of the hours. As much as possible of the entire Bible should be covered, and the entire development seen as a form of continuing the Liturgy of the Word that forms the first portion of our Sunday worship.*

In the final analysis, it has to be admitted that no solution will prove adequate until the entire concept of the Liturgy of the Hours is looked at once again, hopefully before Vatican III or Geneva I is called into being. A major revision is demanded, and nothing less will satisfy the rightful need that God's people has to regain their heritage as those who offer a sacrifice of praise to God.

Editor's Note: The author of this book is the General Editor and author of a bi-monthly publication, *SHARE THE WORD*, which is published by the Paulist National Catholic Center for Evangelization. It offers a popular commentary upon the Sunday readings, together with a guide for group discussions and a closing rite. It also provides daily readings for the weekdays prior to each Sunday, each of which is chosen to relate to the Sunday texts. Within the course of three years, these daily readings provide a guide to the greatest part of the Bible, and serve to center the Sunday celebration as the weekly Easter it truly is.

CHAPTER VI

SACRED SIGNS FOR SACRED DAYS

In our present understanding of the liturgical days, there are certain items that have become identified with particular days. When we think of ashes, Ash Wednesday comes to mind; Passion Sunday marks the beginning of Lent's holiest week, but in the popular mind it is known as Palm Sunday, and if it always centered around the reading of the Passion, our minds still focus on the palms that were blessed and carried; mention of blessed water and candle brings the Easter vigil to mind, wtih Easter water and the Paschal Candle as its principal symbols.

Such objects could be treated separately under "things," for they are what comes to mind as soon as one hears the word "sacramentals." Some have given them the name "The Greater Sacramentals" to distinguish them from other items, for Easter Water is not the same as holy water, and there are many candles used in churches, but none so outstanding as the Paschal Candle. It is their intimate connection with the truly outstanding days of the year that calls for us to consider them in the light of their relevance to sacred time, sacred days and seasons.

In determining the origin of the sacramentals' power to

move our hearts and enlighten our minds, the Church has always spoken of the Paschal Mystery, for it is from the new creation achieved by Christ's death-and-rising that our life in grace finds its source. We can look at these greater signs, then, as significant to our observance of time, as signs of God's intervention in time and in history. Since the Paschal Mystery is the "mother of all feasts," the principal celebration that finds its echoes on each Sunday of the year, we look at the "greater sacramentals" by considering the "Paschal Sacramentals."

ASHES — *Banishment and Exile*

To most minds, ashes are a sign of repentance, and the ancient formula was taken to remind us of the death that faces us all, the frailty of our lives, of which sinfulness is itself the incontestable proof. "Remember, man, that thou art dust, and unto dust thou shalt return." That formula even found its way into funeral rites, in some places, as earth was sprinkled upon the casket (as if any sign other than the casket were needed to remind the bystanders that death was a reality!). Even if the words went on to speak of "sure and certain sign of our resurrection," those words comforted, but forced a meaning not obvious in the earth being used.

Many would search for the significance for ashes within the scriptural account of creation; Adam was formed "out of the clay of the ground" (Gn 2:7), for although there was earth and rain, there was "no man to till the soil" (Gn 2:6). From the dust of the earth, as the story would indicate, there came one to make it a garden. God planted "a garden" in Eden, and Adam would be the groundskeeper, having been part of the ground himself.

The one obvious fact, and a "mystery" (or at least a "puzzle") for people in ancient times, was that the body decayed after death. The "dust" that resulted had to be explained, and so the origin of the body from the "dust" of the earth was accepted by many cultures before this story entered the sacred pages as a part of our salvation's history.

We are, after all, explorers of what puzzles us, and search for meaning in things we notice and cannot understand, especially in those things we cannot master or alter.

Genesis does provide us with the source of symbolism for ashes, but the meaning is traced within the entire story of Adam and Eve, and not simply in the creation of Adam. The fall from grace, for which the planting of the garden prepares the reader, is the end of the story (at least for a while, until new Adam would appear among us), and it is there that the ashes of Wednesday draw their significance.

Originally, the catechumens preparing for Baptism on Easter's night (as Sabbath ended and the day of Resurrection was already beginning to dawn) were accustomed to fast in preparation for that sacrament. Soon, the entire community would join them, fasting and praying with them, and Lent, with its forty days, became a season of preparation for Easter. The history of the rites of reconciliation shows that Lent was to become a time of preparation, by the penitents, for their admission into the community once again. From about the 6th century, Holy Thursday was observed as the day when public sinners were restored to full communion with the Church, and Lent became that time in which their penances were publicly performed. At first, since Sunday could not be a day on which a penitential act could receive proper attention, the following Monday became the day for the rite of assigning the penances. When Lent attained its full completion as a period of forty days, the Wednesday before the first Sunday of Lent was fixed for these rites, as well as the start of the Church's period of fasting and prayer.

The penitents appeared in sackcloth, and ashes were poured upon their heads. The practice had evolved in the East at a much earlier date, and was adopted by the West for this opening day of Lent. The sinners were "banished" from the company of the faithful communicants, and the story of the creation of Adam along with the story of expulsion from the garden were read. A fiery sword was an impractical symbol, but the "dust" of the earth was certainly an available "sign" of this banishment.

Moreover, the sacred scriptures had a wealth of stories about penitents who fasted in sackcloth and ashes: Job (2:8 and 42:6), Daniel (9:3), and the king and people of Nineveh (Jon 3:6), the latter appearing again in the words of Jesus (Mt 11:21). In addition, there was also the reminder that Sodom and Gomorrah, the cities that did not repent of their ways, were "blanketed" with "ashes" (2 Pt 2:6), and were "condemned to destruction" for their sinfulness. The ritual exclusion of the penitents was accompanied by a laying on of hands (sign that they belonged to the Church nonetheless) which was soon attached to the imposition of ashes.

During the 10th century, what was observed for the penitents became a custom for the entire community. All were seen as sinners, and (much to the relief of the penitents, one can be sure) the rite was extended to all. The custom has carried over to our times, certainly as one of the most popular ceremonies of the year, even if not always properly understood. A sense of uncomfortableness with reminders of death (which ashes were never intended to be in the first place) has led to many ingenious ways to keep the symbol and add new meanings. An antiphon now used mentions that we are to "leave the past in ashes," which is clever to say the least.

In addition, there is a second formula for imposition of ashes, one that calls us to true repentance: "Turn away from sin and believe the Good News," which, in effect, tells us to so live the gospel as to give evidence that our faith is real. It will be necesary for the homilist to turn our attention to this facet, while bringing out the significance of the rite. Ashes have a fascinating attraction, and should be used in such a way as to be more than a quaint custom from past tradition, or a symbol overloaded with meanings.

A PASTORAL REFLECTION

With the newer formula, one suggestion can be made. The procession for ashes can be made a true procession, one that moves the participants from one point to another, all within the ambit of the newer words (which should be favored, since ashes have been removed from their setting of banishment with the passing of time). Penitent yet faithful Christians can approach the minister of imposition (drawn from all ministries within the community), and then proceed to the Gospel-Book (one book only, so as not to multiply symbols, and thereby deprive them of significance) to venerate the gospels as a sign of willingness to believe them and live them. The Gospel-Book may rest upon its place of enthronement, surrounded by appropriate lighted tapers, and a simple bow, or other gesture of respect, may be paid to the book. It may also be held by someone, and held out to be kissed; the book should lie open, itself a sign of truth revealed, and perhaps suggestive of our openness to its joyful message.

Some communities may wish to explore a ceremony whereby ashes are made, for the tradition has been to use the palms from the past year to provide ashes for the present year. There can be value to that, especially if done properly. Perhaps, on the Tuesday before Ash Wednesday, this rite of burning the palms can take place for those interested. Some communities have done so, inviting all present to come forward with small pieces of paper on which their failures have been written (or their "successes" recorded as well), to be burned with the ashes. This has a dimension of commitment to it, and one parish made this a preparatory rite for those returning to the Church after an absence of years; it had meaning for them.

There is also one symbolism that can be brought forth as well. Ashes are the residue of fire. We move from ashes to Easter, and ashes look forward to Easter just as fasting anticipates feast, and abstinence reaffirms the value of what could be overlooked as valuable in ordinary usage. Ashes foresee the Paschal Fire, and it is the nature of sacramentals to be signs that foresee.

PALMS — Return and Triumph

If ashes, at the start of Lent, are symbolic of banishment, for the statement about "return to the ground" from which

Adam had been "taken" was spoken after the fall (Gn 3:19), the true symbol of humankind's "return" is found in the palm-branches that mark the beginning of the Great Week we know as "Holy Week." Sinners are called to repentance on the Wednesday of Ashes, but they are reminded that God himself "repented" of his decision to banish and destroy by the celebration of the Sunday of Palms.

The history of God's intervention is marked by what the sacred authors call this "repentance of God" in dealing with his people: the flood devastated the earth, but the waters receded and those on the ark were saved — a new beginning. Adam would be exiled from the garden, but "there was a garden" in "the place" where New Adam "had been crucified" (Jn 19:41); upon seeing him, Mary "supposed he was the gardener" (Jn 20:15), for that was what Adam had been. It was not a natural mistake, but a true "vision" of what was taking place that "first day of the week" (Jn 20:1) — new creation. It was always God's intention that things should be as they were "in the beginning." John's Gospel did not open with that phrase without planned purpose; in a way, it sums up his entire gospel-story.

Very early in the Church's history, the events of the Passion were recalled, and took their shape in that Holy City where the saving event had occurred. By the 4th century, a complete liturgy had evolved, connected with the sites which had witnessed the events. From the beginning, the Sunday of Palms had been connected with the reading of the Passion, and even though the triumphal entry into Jerusalem was reenacted, and palm-branches used, it was the Passion that lent its coloring and even its title to this day.

Within the Hebrew Scriptures those branches were signs of new beginning, and with a notion of "return." Leviticus sets down the rule that the Feast of Booths be celebrated each year, to recall that God "led the Israelites *out* of Egypt" and "made them dwell in booths" (Lv 23:43). To celebrate this return from exile, the people were enjoined to "gather foliage from majestic trees, branches of palms and boughs of myrtle,...and then for a week" to "keep this pilgrim feast of the Lord" (Lv 23:40,41). "They kept the feast for seven days, and the solemn assembly on the eighth day, as was required" (Neh 8:18). Accordingly, the writer of the Fourth Gospel can say that "the crowd that had come for the feast . . . got palm branches" as they came out to meet the Lord (Jn 12:13), and although the celebration was Passover, the allusion to the Feast of Booths is there, not in subtlety alone, but in nuance and recall.

From the 4th century, the pilgrim Egeria has provided us with a complete description of events as celebrated in Jerusalem. Bethany became the place where Christians gathered on the eve of Sunday, to commemorate the supper held in the house of Simon the Leper. By Sunday, the community gathered on the Mount of Olives, and towards evening the gospel-account of the Lord's triumphal entry was read, and a procession formed. It made its way into Jerusalem to the Church of the Resurrection, where the Passion was read, and evening praise took place.

Her account was penned for those back in Gaul, and eventually made its way into Rome and into the Roman liturgy. It has marked the basis for these rites ever since, and this Sunday of the Lord's Passion observed a procession, sign of "pilgrim feast," that marked the Lord's "return" to his city. In some areas, as the liturgy (or liturgies) took shape, the procession gave due respect to the "greeting" of the Lord. A place, or church, was designated "a little Bethany," where palms were blessed, and from there the community could process to the principal church of the city, now viewed as "a little Jerusalem." It is the movement of the people, together with their carrying of palm-branches, that combined to form one symbolic event. Sometimes the Book of Gospels was brought in procession to represent Christ; in Rouen, the Sacrament of the altar was removed on Saturday night, and carried in solemn procession on Sunday; and in Bavaria, a sculpture of Jesus on a donkey (the "palmesel") was placed on rollers, coming at the end of the procession. All were attempts to convey a sense that the past was present in their celebration, and not simply a recalling of this Sunday's events; redemption was being re-lived.

Later development only added symbol to symbol, in an effort to assure that all the aspects of this day would be signified. In our century, the celebrant would stand outside the church with the people, and knock on the doors with the foot of the processional cross, an element that was removed in the reforms of 1955. It did have something to say about the full meaning behind this day. The Lord had "suddenly" come back to his city, to repossess it. Just as the Feast of Booths recalled a "return" from Banishment, so too had the great exile (when Jerusalem was destroyed in the 6th century before Christ) come to its end, and God had returned to the city where he had dwelt among his people. Since sacramentals are *signs that foresee*, this ceremony looked to that coming day when the Lord would return once again, and take possession of his "city," the Church.

A PASTORAL REFLECTION

All the rich theology of this day can be brought to the fore without the multiplication of symbols. Multiplication had its meaning with loaves and fishes, as it does with grace and graces, but symbols multiplied tend to vie with one another in our minds as though in competition.

The procession that marks "a pilgrim feast" is essential to this Sunday, and should never be omitted, despite the tolerance of rubrics for lesser rites; less is never more when an essential ingredient is overlooked. There should be separate places, from where the people can move to another place. It would be ideal in the minds of many for *separate communities* (and that term can be defined in its fullest meaning) to exchange sites. If this can be done separately from the Mass of the Passion, that will only allow for the celebration of the Passion to regain its proper emphasis for this day.

At the very least, let there be movement. Banishment from Eden marked a sad "procession" of sorts, and our "exile" has come to an end. "We have here no lasting city." Abraham journeyed "as in a foreign country, dwelling in tents . . . looking forward to the city . . . whose designer and maker is God" (Heb 11:9,10), which can be seen as eternal Jerusalem or this earth of ours come to its full stature.

And let there be "foliage," not meager slips of palm.

Throughout Lent, as the tradition has been, an absence of growing things should mark the adornment of the church. After all, it was from the "garden" that we see Adam and Eve expelled. As this Sunday looks to the "eighth day" as the "solemn assembly" begun this day, we will be prepared to see the "gardener" as did Mary, especially if green and growth are present to lend another sign that a festival of seven days has now begun.

As the Community moves to its "solemn assembly on the eighth day," which Passion Sunday of the Palms inaugurated, the church can begin to heighten its anticipation of Easter joy even as it recalls Passion and Death. Trees (especially the palm) can provide a setting that carries the symbolism of the Lord's entry through the entire week. The carrying of branches to honor their Lord is of itself a sign that the community of believers is the true "booth" or tent-of-meeting in which God has chosen to dwell with his people; the building itself can remind us of what we are and were always meant to be.

HOLY OILS — Gladness and Strength

To a people accustomed to making use of the elements of earth as signs of deeper and divine realities, the praying of the 23rd Psalm takes on a dimension which transfers the symbolism into a lived experience. "You anoint my head with oil" (Ps 23:5) has meaning different from that the psalmist knew; but for the follower of Christ, anointed at baptism, sealed in the Spirit, ordained to ministry, or/and anointed during illness, the experience itself allows the phrase to speak in a different way than as the recalling of a way of life lost in history.

Like bread and wine, oil was a staple of life in ancient times (as it is today, when one thinks about cholesterol and cooking, or perfumes and lotions). When Ishmael came to Gedaliah, the people were able to have their lives spared by pointing out where "the stores" of "wheat and oil" had been buried (Jer 41:8). Because it was ordinary, it was received as something extraordinary, a blessing from God; it was only natural, therefore, that oil be given a role in the ceremonies of worship.

Israel's kings were anointed with oil, as was David (1 Chr 11:3), as were her priests, with oil poured "on the head" (Ex 29:7). The pouring out of oil, sign of one's wealth richly poured out, or spilled before God, marked the special blessing of places and things; when Jacob had his dream, the famous "Jacob's ladder" vision, he recognized the site as holy, "an abode of God," and marked the place by taking the stone on which his head had rested, and making it "a memorial stone," pouring "oil on top of it" (Gn 28:17,19).

Oil would retain its significance as water changed to wine, to borrow John's symbolism, and former covenant became new testament. The word "Christ" means "anointed." Jesus of Nazareth is the one whom God had "anointed with the Holy Spirit and power" (Acts 10:38). His followers can be described as those who have received "the anointing that comes from the Holy One" (1 Jn 2:20), an "anointing that teaches" (1 Jn 2:27), for it is the Spirit who will "instruct" us "in everything" (Jn 14:26).

It was only natural that oil be viewed as a sacred sign to Christ's followers, and that Paul can say "Christ" it is "who anointed us and has sealed us, thereby depositing . . . the Spirit in our hearts" (2 Cor 1:21-22). That this truth should receive visible significance by the use of oil does not surprise us. Given our view of creation as redeemed and being transformed, it would surprise us if oil were not used.

Since baptism was conferred at the vigil of Easter, and anointings were so important to those rites, the preparation of holy oils began to take place prior to Easter. It was a purely practical matter, and the rich symbolism of the oil itself would call out for special attention. Since Jesus was "anointed" at the house of Simon "six days before Passover" (Jn 12:1), the blessing of oils was early fixed for Holy Week apart from pure necessity. It was not long before Holy Thursday was set for the eucharistic celebration in which the bishop and his clergy gathered to consecrate the oils to be used in the sacramental rites of the Church.

In the course of time, three oils were to emerge from ceremonies and usage: a special oil (chrism) for anointing of persons to ministry (later, of kings to their state); oil of catechumens, for the anointings at baptism; and oil of the sick, for the rites of anointing those who were ill. Exodus (30:22-33) describes the elaborate preparation of the "sacred anointing oil," the "perfumed ointment expertly prepared." (The notion of *perfumed* oil would itself become a sign of the "aroma of Christ" which "we are," spreading "the fragrance of his knowledge" everywhere we go; 2 Cor 2:14,15). The Church's rites for the consecration of oils would take on this solemnity with the development of years, and with a growing appreciation of its sacramental importance (to Baptism, Confirmation, Holy Orders and Anointing of the Sick).

The revision of the rites of Holy Week have restored the "Mass of Chrism" to its earlier status as a rite separate from the other celebrations of Holy Thursday (reconciliation of penitents, and the Lord's Supper) that are special to that day. It has been suggested that another day be chosen, close to Easter, and at a time that allows as many as possible to take part in these rites.

A PASTORAL REFLECTION

The holy oils came to be seen as "a vessel" of the Spirit's presence. Prepared within the sanctuary of the cathedral itself, venerated by bishops and clergy together, carried in procession while a hymn is sung, in which the "fruit of the olive tree" (recalling the olive branch carried to Noah's ark by the dove) was seen as "bringing the promises of the peace of Christ" the Lord, the oils were placed in a special area of the church, and placed in containers for use throughout the diocese.

The cathedral church should be the place of celebration, the place where the entire people comes together to see they are not merely local communities, but a body extended in every place. Perhaps those to be baptized and confirmed could be present (or at least represented) since this rite is connected with the Easter sacraments, and have an active part, especially in their preparing of the oils, and in their accompanying them from the sanctuary. The ministry to the sick (to include the professionals who assist the ill in hospitals and clinics) should be present and active in the rite of blessing the oil of the sick.

Once the oils are returned to the local communities, might it not be possible for them to "welcome" these signs of what we are? The "ambry," usually located in the sacristy, might better have its location within the church proper, and not as some convenient little hole-in-the-wall more overlooked than noticed. The oils are always a sign of what we are, the Lord's anointed ones. A dialogue of prayer, in which the words of blessing alternate between bishop and people (with each oil consecrated by him and those for whom that particular oil has greater significance) might mark the future rites of blessing. Altars are consecrated, as are sacred vessels, and so are persons, all believers; all, no less than tables of worship and sacred vessels, are worthy of being seen as anointed ones, after the pattern of the Christ, the Anointed One.

WASHING OF FEET — Heritage and Service

Holy Thursday has been known as "Maundy Thursday," after the Latin word *mandatum*, referring to the great "command," the mandate to "wash each other's feet" (Jn 13:14). What the Teacher and Lord did, as he washed the feet of his disciples, was to set an example to be followed. The Church seems to have viewed this activity as a parable acted out, rather than as an imperative to be reenacted.

There is not much evidence in liturgical history that this rite was universally practiced, or that it formed part of the observance of the Holy Triduum, the three days, excluding Easter, that surrounded the Paschal Mystery. We see it emerge as part of the ceremonies of initiation in Milan, for it was seen as a suitable ceremony for those becoming disciples of the Lord with their baptism into him. From there it was adopted by other churches, and finally made its way into the liturgy of Holy Thursday, where it has remained to this day. With the revision of the liturgy for Holy Week in 1955, and the recent revision of our rites, it has once again received its proper prominence . That it was prominent in the early Church can not be doubted, for until the setting of the number of the sacraments as seven, the washing of the feet had been considered by some to be a sacrament.

John's Gospel mentions no account of the institution of the Eucharist, and this opening incident from all that took place on the night before Jesus died, was seen in relation to the giving of the Eucharist which the other Gospels record. It is a parable that foresees the complete gift of self which was to be made within the course of events which followed. Jesus would lay his garments aside, wash his disciples' feet, and put his garments on again; in a similar way, he would lay his role as God's Son aside, assume the role of a servant, and having gained their cleansing by his own death, would reappear as Son of God, robed in glory.

A PASTORAL REFLECTION

Until the revision of the liturgical rites, this ceremony suffered from neglect, a custom more honored in the breach than in the observance. There are some who still think that this gesture of humility does not "speak" to today's generation. But it is an acted sign that *recalls* what Jesus did, *declares* him servant, *obliges* us to serve, and *foresees* the day when that notion of service will be the privileged duty of every member of the Church.

In one parish, where a rite of reconciliation takes place for those returning to the Church, the community welcomes them back by washing their feet. Their feet are washed, not only by celebrant, but by members of the council and members of the community at large. For them, as representatives of the parish, the gesture speaks not only to those who are now reconciled, but to the community itself; sometimes the estrangement from the Church is a result of the failure of the Church to respond to needs, and to provide for faith's support.

The rite of footwashing, when extended to cover other ministries, can serve as an example of what it means to serve. By having other ministers, and other members, "concelebrate" this rite, perhaps the day will be advanced when the participation of all in the ministry of the Church will see deeper acknowledgement; the participation of others, who serve the human family, can also speak, to them as to us, that the world is being transformed, and that ours is a redeemed creation.

THE CROSS — *Curse Removed, Victory Assured*

It is Paul who sums up best our approach to the cross. He who could say that he was "crucified with Christ" (Gal 2:20), with him who "was displayed to view upon his cross" (Gal 3:1), was able to proclaim: "May I never boast of anything but the cross of our Lord Jesus Christ," for by it he was "created anew" (Gal 6:14,15). He could present the image of the cross, and "speak of nothing but Jesus Christ and him crucified" (1 Cor 2:2), calling the death of Christ before his reader's eyes, and it would have an impact not present to our day. As he preached and wrote, the cross was still being used; the Roman means of execution would not await him, for he was a citizen of the Empire, and would be granted the "privilege" of being put to death by the sword. His death, nonetheless, would be his ultimate way of dying with the Lord.

The early Church did not make use of the cross as a symbol, for it evoked painful memories, memories we would associate with any instrument of execution. When the cross came to be used as symbol, it was in disguised form. The imagery would recall a tree, with all the associations from scripture that could be made. In Acts, Peter is seen referring to the cross, describing how Jesus was "put to death, hanging . . . on a tree" (Acts 5:30). The use of "tree" to describe the cross brought association with the Law of

Moses, where it stands written: "God's curse rests on him who hangs on a tree" (Dt 21:23). Paul saw, in the cross of Christ, freedom from observances of the Law. Since the Lord Jesus was delivered from death by "hanging on a tree" and rising to life again, so all who would find themselves "cursed" for not abiding by the law (Gal 3:10) are similarly delivered.

If the "tree" of the cross represents freedom from such a "curse," the Church perceived that this "tree" also delivered us from the "curse" of banishment from Eden. The early hymns that honor the cross see the "Tree" that is the cross restoring humankind to that innocence which it had before Adam and Eve "ate from the tree" in Eden (Gn 3:17). As the prefaces to the Eucharistic Prayer affirm: Jesus "triumphed over Satan's pride," and the "tree" which marked human defeat has become "the tree of victory."

The earliest representations of the cross were emblems of this victory. Not until the 6th century do we find a representation of Jesus, usually in the symbolism of "the Lamb" appearing in front of the cross, and not actually affixed to it. When the human figure was depicted, it also appeared before the cross, standing in front of it, fully clothed and often wearing a crown of glory. The 11th century saw the beginnings of our present-day crucifix, Jesus being "fixed" to the cross, and the attitude of suffering and death began to replace the attitude and posture of triumph.

Devotion to the cross took its liturgical form at least by the 7th century, but as a veneration of a relic of the true cross. The precious fragment of wood was preserved in a special casque, brought to the altar, and left there throughout the service on Good Friday. The service was soon introduced by having the pope "unveiling" this relic, kissing it, and the other clergy then joined him in venerating this relic. The custom spread as the Roman liturgy was adopted by other churches, with a wooden cross being used in place of a relic, for such fragments were increasingly rare. In time, the practice of veiling the cross was to be a commonplace, beginning in the last weeks of Lent (which unfortunately began to be seen as a season of its own, Passiontide). Statues were also covered, for the saints were signs of the glory yet to come, and any emblem of triumph was hidden from sight, as devotion to the passion of Christ grew.

A PASTORAL REFLECTION

The cross (or crucifix) has become a necessary part of the furnishings of the sanctuary. Some have assumed monumental proportions, and few represent the victory that it represents, but glory flowed from death, and a reminder of that saving death should not be absent. Both elements, death and life, met at that tree, and both should be brought to mind.

If care is taken to have that cross becoming to the liturgy, and noble in its simplicity, the sanctuary cross should be the cross used at the "veneration" of Good Friday. If it can not be removed, and brought in with a solemn procession, the adoration of the sanctuary cross can take part by having all kneel and adore in silence. The use of another cross simply multiplies the symbolism, and detracts from it.

The custom of veiling the cross has been abandoned, but it had its value. It set the mood for these solemn days, and perhaps that practice can be rethought. The cross can be draped, however, so that attention is focused on this primary symbol of our freedom, and the draping closed prior to the beginning of the Sacred Triduum, which begins on the evening of Holy Thursday. The cross is "the banner of the king," and cloth that enfolds makes of the cross a banner.

WATER — New Creation and Cleansing

The arid climate of the Holy Land gave to water an importance that is often overlooked, or taken for granted by many of us. It is a commonplace of life for most of us, and this in itself would suggest that it is special; its special nature, however, derives from its being appreciated.

The role that water played throughout salvation history would require a separate chapter, if not an entire book. The blessing of water at Easter recalls "the dawn of creation," the flood, the Red Sea, the coming into a land of promise by crossing the Jordan, Ezekiel's vision of abundant water flowing from the temple, etc. Add to such events the Baptism of Christ, the water changed to wine, the Lord's own symbolism of Holy Spirit as "fountain" that wells up from within, and the "water" that flowed from his side (Jn 19:34), and the importance of the element of water becomes obvious.

The blessing of water became one of the earliest rites of the Church's worship, and the fact that the Easter Vigil was devoted to the celebration of Baptism led to the formal blessing of the water that would be used in this rite. Its intimate connection with this sacrament caused it to be used as a reminder of baptism itself. Holy water was eventually to mark the entrances of our churches, so that each could recall her or his baptism upon arriving for worship, and the sprinkling with water would become a rite that marked the beginning of Mass (at least on Sundays) for many centuries. In the present revision, the blessing and sprinkling of water is one form of the introductory rites.

A PASTORAL REFLECTION

The importance of blessed water led to its being used for other rites of blessing, in particular the blessing of homes. But its primary use is the recalling of our baptism. In many of our churches today, the baptismal font has been placed not at the entrance (where it stood as a reminder that one "entered" the Church through this sacrament of initiation), but within the body of the church, enabling the entire community to participate in the rites. The use of this font, as members enter for worship, and individually recall their baptismal commitment, can only serve to be a great help in making one aware that baptism is not a moment but a constancy, not a rite but a way of life.

If individual fonts are used at entrances, they might resemble the font without duplicating that font, either in the materials used, or in the form they assume. At funerals, when the Easter (or blessed) water is used, again recalling baptism, the baptismal font (prominently seen by all) should be approached, either by celebrant or member of the family, and that water sprinkled over the casket, and brought to the gravesite so that all might better appreciate its symbolism of new life achieved by saving death.

PASCHAL CANDLE — Pillar of Fire, Light For All

If one symbol were to be chosen to serve as Easter's representative, the Paschal Candle must be chosen. The associations with all of salvation's history are too numerous for light to be overlooked. The Paschal Candle, apart from recalling Jesus as "the light of the world" (Jn 8:12), that arose from the darkness of the tomb "while it was still dark" (Jn 20:1), recalls the events of creation and deliverance that have served to signify the Paschal Mystery as creation's deliverance.

Light marks the first element of creation itself, when God said "Let there be light," and "there was light" (Gn 1:3). At that moment, "God separated the light from the darkness" (Gn 1:4). The lighting of the new fire, the lighting of the Easter candle, recalls not only the creation of light, but its being "separated" from the darkness, "a darkness that did not overcome it" (Jn 1:5). At the Exodus of Israel from Egypt, when God's people began to be formed as a nation, "separated" from a state of slavery, that creation and separation was summed up as the Lord "preceded them . . . at night by means of a pillar of fire to give them light" (Ex 13:21). At the Easter Vigil, the people "created" by baptism proceed behind a waxen "pillar of fire," and their very movement suggests deliverance, pilgrimage with the Risen One who goes before us, even as the Gospel of Mark records that he was "going ahead of" disciples into Galilee, where they would "see him just as he told" them (Mk 16:7).

Most likely the Paschal Candle traces its origins back to the *lucernarium*, the lighting of lights that was marked by psalms and prayers, to be known as vespers or Evening

Prayer. Deacons were in charge of lighting these evening lights for this hour of prayer, and the role of a deacon in the ceremonies of the Easter Vigil has been preserved throughout the centuries. That rite can be traced back to the 8th century as part of the Easter celebration.

The obvious symbolism of the candle led to its being blessed, and to its decoration.

Holy and Glorious Wounds

The cross began to be traced upon the candle itself, so that the candle became a "cross," an emblem of passion. Grains of incense would next be used, to mark the five wounds. (Their use is a curious thing, for such large grains of resin, rough yet sparkling, suggested "scabs" where nails and spear left their trace.) Eventually wax "nails," encasing grains of incense, were to be used instead, a practice still employed at present.

Great importance was attached to this feature, the same importance that John's Gospel gives them. Thomas saw the Risen One, the very same Jesus of Nazareth whom the world saw displayed upon the cross. What he saw, behind doors that were locked, the disciples of all time behold when viewing the Paschal Candle. That waxed pillar, marked by "holy and glorious wounds" (words used in preparing the candle), serves the same function as the gospel narative — to "help" us believe that "Jesus" who died, rose as "Messiah," and that "through this faith" we may have "life" (Jn 20:31).

As a symbol associated with time, the candle is also associated with timelessness. The numerals for the current years are traced in the four angles which the cross forms, and an alpha and omega is traced, one atop, the other below, this cross. Jesus is "Alpha and Omega, the beginning and the end" (Rev 21:6).

A PASTORAL REFLECTION

Until recently, the Paschal Candle stood in the sanctuary, and was extinguished on Ascension Thursday, immediately after the reading of the gospel at Mass. This was seen as making of the symbolism a sign of the "earthly days" of Jesus, and so the custom was ended. The Paschal Candle stands where it does until Pentecost, and is now carried to the baptismal font, where it remains, a sign of Easter triumph "presiding" at every baptism to take place there.

The candle itself should be imposing, and utterly simple, unadorned with flowers and other "symbols." It is a symbol in and of itself, and so should be allowed to speak for itself. The cross, with numerals, with "nails," and with the alpha and omega, are adornment aplenty. If not lit during the entire season, it should be lit throughout the time when worship will take place, and other candles draw their flame from Easter's fire.

At funerals, the cross can be used in procession at the welcoming of the body. When the rites of commendation and farewell are finished, the Paschal Candle (which can remain in its permanent place, if it can be easily seen by all) is carried, and thus forms the start of the procession from the church, with all its recall of "passing-over" from death to life. Its *movement* is the principal sign here, not simply its presence. The casket might simply rest before the altar without the candle in front of it, for the casket, clothed in white, takes on its own symbolism.

PART THREE

THE SACREDNESS OF PLACE

People and nations have their special places, locations that say here, and not there. We exist under a "territorial imperative" that requires us to fix the boundaries to our lives, to settle the limits of those areas that define who we are and what we do. The child is told where to go and where not to go, and the child within us continues to select places to visit, revisit, or avoid. Certain places speak to us as no others can, and speak for themselves without our having to speak for them, or giving them "names" so that others will learn what we know or imagine. Anyplace can have its own sense of being set apart, different than any other place, even though it may have something different to say to those who come or tarry there.

Like holy places, like the sacramentals we call churches, shrines and cemeteries, locations *recall* a past, *declare* a present, *oblige* a commitment, and *foresee* a future, or at least a possibility. Those that have the greatest significance are capable of achieving all these elements. It can be as simple a matter as visiting our birthplace, or our childhood home, or as important an event as standing in awe before the Magna Carta or the Constitution, or reverently visiting the Tomb of the Unknown Soldier.

Places *recall* the past, and are identified with beginnings, whether our own or those of our nation. They take on added meaning simply because they define where we began. Nations have enshrined their history in terms of sites where this or that took place; we can think in terms of a country's borders, but we do so within the confines of this or that place where the nation began. Even if a modern building now stands where a large city once began, and only a small plaque marks the spot, the new identifies the former.

Places *declare* their own truth, and provide their own environment. One enters the halls of Congress, or the Supreme Court, and silence seems natural, as though to let the buildings have their say. Even the magnificence is but an effort to fashion a minor world within, a "world" that is different from all that is outside. Were one to visit Washington, taking in all the sights and sites, and come at day's waning to Arlington, and the simple grave of Robert Kennedy, one could not fail to be impressed by the simplicity of a simple wooden cross that says "here" and not "there," or "elsewhere."

Places *oblige* us to rethink our own positions. Sites where we are standing force us to ponder where we stand on issues, and the same place may find a variety of stances being taken. Battlesites do more than recall victories for those attuned to hear echoes of the dead and wounded; they enjoin a recommitment for patriot and peacemaker alike, even if the one who stands there is both patriot and peacemaker.

And places *foresee* to those with vision. A tract of land is future home for a couple or a corporation, and a possibility for productionist and preservationist alike. What is, points to what can be, or will be. Exploration leads to discovery, and hopefully to rediscovery. During the Second World War, as so many places were being devastated, T.S. Eliot, in *Little Gidding*, a poem that takes a place for its name, could write:

> "We shall not cease from exploration
> And the end of all our exploring
> Will be to arrive where we started
> And know the place for the first time."

One can trace this truth within salvation's history. "The heavens and the earth and all their array" (Gn 2:1) seem to have been compressed to "a garden," and pin-pointed, as it were, to a "tree in the middle of the garden" (Gn 3:3). It was from that garden that "the man and his wife" were "expelled," and "settled" just "east of Eden" (Gn 3:24). With the "revolving" sword of fire to guard its entrance, return would be impossible. From that moment on, one could say, the history of humankind has been an attempt to relocate the garden, to recreate an Eden, since return was impossible. As the sacred story ends, we read of "God's dwelling," whose "gates shall never be shut" (Rv 21:25), with a river that watered "the trees of life" (Rv 22:2), the new Eden, from which none shall be banished once entrance has been gained.

Between Genesis and Revelation, however, one traces the efforts to establish the link between God and his creation, and to undo the myth that God had banished himself from his own work. We see Jacob coming to "a certain shrine" (Gn 28:12), where he has a dream of "a stairway" reaching between heaven and earth. Upon awaking, he realizes that "the Lord is in this spot" (Gn 28:16), and taking the stone, once part of the shrine, he "set it up as a memorial stone" (Gn 28:18), giving the place its name of Bethel, the "house of God." The Israelites will call a place Taberah, because "there the fire of the Lord burned among them" (Nm 11:3), and name another place Kibroth-hattavah since "it was there that the greedy people were buried" (Nm 11:34). This is more than an attempt to explain the meaning of familiar names for places; it is an effort to identify those places with the presence of God, whether visited by his presence, as at Bethel, or by his wrath, as at Taberah.

Perhaps that truth stands out most clearly when Moses saw "fire flaming out of a bush," drew near in his wonder at the sight, and was told: "Come no nearer! Remove the sandals from your feet, for the place where you stand is holy ground" (Ex 3:1-5). Elizabeth Barrett Browning could recall the scene, and comment that "Earth's crammed with heaven, And every common bush afire with God." Sometimes we need to hear the delightful story of Naaman, the Aramean commander of the army, healed of his leprosy, and begging to take "two mule-loads of earth" back to his home, that he might worship the God of Israel in a land that knew other gods.

In defining sacred space, we affirm that all the earth is holy ground. It is still "very good," a redeemed creation, and if sin spoils the vision, it does not alter the fact. In stating that one place is "holy ground," we do not deny that all ground is holy, nor affirm that the profane has been expelled from the sacred. The holiness we attribute to one place affirms the sacredness of every place, which is why we can call our churches "sacramentals."

CHAPTER VII

A SACRED SPACE

In the revealed religion found in Hebrew Scriptures and New Testament, we encounter the God who intervened in the world he had fashioned. No need to dream of Mount Olympus, peopled with gods and goddesses, but Sinai and Golgotha, where people encountered God. If other religions built their temples in an effort to enshrine a god, and hold divinity captive, as it were, the religion of Israel, which moved from many "high places" to "Zion" as God's "resting place," proclaimed the God whom heaven and earth could not contain. The author of Hebrews could still affirm that Abraham "sojourned in the promised land as in a foreign country," as though "looking forward to the city . . . whose designer and maker is God" (Heb 11:9,10).

Commanded to "make a sanctuary" for their God, the people of Israel erected their tent of meeting, to know that God was dwelling "in their midst" (Ex 25:8). Later, that dwelling-place would be the temple in Jerusalem. It was there that God was worshiped, his psalms sung with festive dance, and sacrifices offered according to the Law.

When the Fourth Gospel spoke of a new "beginning," and the opening hymn described the Incarnation, it would be in terms that evoked a tent of meeting. "The Word became flesh and made his dwelling among us" (Jn 1:14); that is,

God *pitched his tent*, which is what the Greek conveys. God's "life became visible," to be "heard" and "seen," "looked upon" and "touched" (1 Jn 1:1,2). For those who would come to believe in him, here was God's dwelling place among us. In speaking of the temple being destroyed, and raised up, we learn that "he was talking about the temple of his body" (Jn 2:21).

When Jesus met the woman at Shechem, she brought up the subject of sacred places. Her ancestors "worshiped on this mountain," she declared, while the Jews "claim that Jerusalem is the place" (Jn 4:20). "Neither on this mountain, nor in Jerusalem," Jesus replies, but "in Spirit and truth" for "authentic worshipers" (Jn 4:21,23). Luke would convey the same truth, in his story about ten lepers. "One of them" returned and "threw himself on his face at the feet of Jesus and spoke his praises" (Lk 17:15,16). Jesus is seen as *the place* where God is worshiped.

This identification with the person and mystery of the Christ reaches its most perfected form in the words which Luke has Stephen say: "The Most High does not dwell in buildings made by human hands" (Acts 7:48). An appeal is made to Isaiah's own words, which acknowledge that "the heavens" are God's "throne," and "the earth" is his "footstool" (Is 66:1).

The Church as Building

If Paul can write the "temple of God is holy," he can immediately add that "you are that temple" (1 Cor 3:17). It is a reaffirmation of Matthew's vision, which holds that "where two or three are gathered" in the name of Jesus, the Lord is "in their midst" (Mt 18:20). For that to take place, a place is needed; there has to be a location "where" the "two or three" can gather, or the two or three hundred, for that matter.

The use of a place is a matter of sheer necessity, and while the first Christians continued to pray in the temple or in synagogues, they met in their homes to celebrate the Lord's

Supper. One finds it hard to imagine that the largest room would not be used, the place reserved for special guests and occasions. Even as the gospel message continued to spread beyond the confines of the holy land, private homes continued in use for some time, "house-churches" in the fullest sense of the term. But larger buildings were needed, and were built, even during times of persecution.

Only when the Church emerged from a world that seemed to have no more room for it (than it had for the Lord at his birth) did the building of places of worship become the commonly accepted practice. Just as one particular day came to be identified as "the Lord's day," so a particular building became known as "the Lord's house." (The Greek word, *kyriake*, would lend itself to our present-day "church.") The *basilica*, or civil hall, would become the perfect place for Christian worship, and the starting-point for church architecture, especially in the West.

In a way, now that the Church had "room," the buildings used for worship reflected a roominess, a spaciousness in which the worshipers could move about freely. The semicircular apse became a *sanctuary*, with a chair for the presiding bishop, and seats for the clergy on each side. Standing free, facing both clergy and the rest of the membership, stood the altar, a table of modest proportions, before which the people stood, with no seats or benches in neat rows (as later development would see).

For the main, church architecture developed with the art of building itself. New forms of architecture led to new forms of churches. The original slanted roof of the early basilicas would become vaulted roofs; Roman arches would be an inspiration and a practical means of support, and the style known as Romanesque came into being. As walls became less massive, and the roof came to rest on vaults, which carried the weight down to the ground itself, more room for windows resulted. The Renaissance era looked upon the newer style as barbaric, like the Goths who once ravaged the land, and called the newer architecture "gothic;" it remains to this day as the most popular form for churches.

Succeeding generations, each building on the past, saw newer styles emerge, and the building known as "a church" reflected the Church's own self-image. With decreasing participation on the part of the people, and the emergence of the clergy as a distinct (and often separate) group, the sanctuaries became the focus of attention and adornment, and the "body" of the church filled with seats, as though for an audience. Even the style of architecture marked the Church's understanding of its role, and a growing sense of "The Church Militant" led to an overpowering, almost triumphant, style of building.

A HOLY LAND

There were other factors, of course, that aided the development of church architecture down to the present. Perhaps the most important lies in the Holy Land itelf. The places associated with the life and ministry of Jesus were too important to be overlooked. Pilgrimages and crusades alike led to each and every church being viewed as "a holy land," holy ground in terms of the places where Jesus walked, suffered, died and rose. As the liturgical year was to take on the aspect of following the earthly career of Jesus, so too did church buildings assume this same attitude and approach.

Those unable to go to Jerusalem, or to any of the sites connected with the life of Christ, were to find certain churches (in time, all churches) marked as "stations" which marked the journeying of Jesus. The "Way of the Cross" would no longer be a route along Jerusalem's streets, but a path within each church with "stations" to guide the "pilgrim" at prayer. Calvary would be symbolized by altars built upon steps, and the crucifix often monumental in proportion. Even the simple tabernacle would receive unusual treatment, leading to an extraordinary piety that saw it a place of reposition, much like the sepulchre where the lifeless body of Jesus was laid to rest.

The church building provides the setting for worship, and if worship became something participated in by few, and only witnessed by all others, one can readily understand why the "sanctuary" took on the appearance of a stage, with people confined to seats arranged in rows. (The story of someone leaving a theatre, and genuflecting at the end of the row before turning to leave, is not a fabrication.) With the revision of our forms of worship there came the need to redefine the space for worship. A simple renovation of the building, even according to the best norms, does not assure a rethinking of attitudes on the part of the assembly gathered for worship. But even a renovation bespeaks renewal, and a rearrangement of space within a church becomes symbol of the renewal taking place within the Church.

A HOUSE FOR THE CHURCH

In the building of new churches, and in the renovation of older buildings, the Church's self-understanding of its mission and role has things to say within the realm of artist and architect, as within the realm of all members of the *ecclesia*, the sacred assembly. It is the Church that gathers within the building, making of it a church. It is the "house of the Lord" itself that meets, coming together within a building that must provide not only the setting for that truth, but its very symbol as well. The church becomes the "sacramental" of the Church, a building "set apart" by its very usage. That the building may achieve its purpose, it may well display the traditional "marks" of the Church, credal formulations made visible in honor of God, maker of all things, "of all that is seen and unseen."

1. The church should be "one," a unified and unifying space.

If the Church is "a sign and instrument of communion with God and of unity among all," as the Dogmatic Constitution on the Church (Art. 1) affirms, the building in which the Church assembles should be no less a sign and instrument of unity.

— The church should be *one* with its environment, part

and partner of the neighborhood in which it is located, even while being "set apart" from other buildings.

— The church should be *one* in its form, without conflicting styles of architecture, and one in its integration of exterior and interior. The outside should honestly convey a sense of what the inside is like.

— The church should be *one* with the age in which it is built, the past summing up a heritage, the present addressing itself to people of the present. A slavish rebuilding of "churchy" buildings bespeaks an inability to be alive, and some of the buildings we have erected resemble the mule, with neither a pride of ancestry nor a promise of posterity. Older churches can be renovated in a way that is true to the architecture of the past and the needs of the present, provided that liturgists and architects can be allowed to freely dialogue with each other and the communities for whom they act as servants.

— The church should be *one* in its ability to do away with needless distinctions, and allow each member of the assembly to assume the proper role of a participant. The different ministries involved in worship (celebrant, eucharistic minister, lector, cantor, "usher" or minister of hospitality, etc.) serve the entire community. The distinction that is theirs as servants is addressed to assuring that all members are actively present as the Body of Christ.

Confining liturgical actions to one space alone establishes a division between ministers and congregation. There should be several places set aside for different functions, so that the entire interior space is seen as a unity. Areas designated for more personal prayer, such as the reservation of the Sacrament of the Altar, even if distant from the Altar, must be integrated with the entire inner space. A similarity of materials can accomplish this, as can the use of color.

— The church should be so arranged that all can see and hear one another, and not merely those who lead them in worship. There should be ample space for movement and gestures, for true signs of peace and full processions, the latter an important sign that we are a pilgrim people.

— The church should be so arranged, either with a foyer or other gathering-place, where all can greet one another, spend time together, share refreshments and conversation, etc., so that a true sense of community can become apparent. It is a natural outflowing of the unity which the liturgy itself fosters and makes present.

2. The church should be "holy," conveying a sense of awe in God's presence.

In our worship, we experience the mystery of God, who is faithful in all his words and holy in all his works" (Ps 145:13). The liturgy centers around the *words* (Scripture) and the *works* (Sacred Actions, Sacraments) of God, and the church should be so constructed as to allow both to be appreciated to the fullest extent possible.

— Every care must be taken to allow the Word of God to be heard, as well as our own words which are response to that Word, whether sung or simply spoken. Any space which deadens sound takes the life out of liturgy as well. If amplification is necessary, since so few churches seem to have been built with an awareness of the science of acoustics, it should be ample, as the very name suggests. Electronic "speakers" should accomplish what the human speakers strive to do — allow each to hear with clarity and ease. In allocating costs, this need is essential, and halfway measures are unacceptable.

— Every care must be taken to assure that the liturgical actions, the *works* of God, be done in an atmosphere that is reverent. A celebrant's careless gestures are perceived as an intrusion into worship; inferior workmanship, tawdry vestments, garish art and untuned instruments are equally ineffective in creating, and sustaining an atmosphere that is reverent and awe-inspiring.

To be "holy" is to be "wholly" in accord with one's own

being and nature. Wood is wood, and not marble, and wooden altars that have been "marbleized" (to take but one example) are poor signs of the sacred; they reinforce the false notion that holiness is a veneer. As in the world, so in the church building: let what is speak for itself, for only then can we perceive that we, too, must be authentic before our God.

3. The church should be "catholic," reflecting an universality of time and place.

If "nothing that is genuinely human fails to find an echo in the hearts of the followers of Christ," then nothing should be excluded from human work and art within the building that houses the Church. That same conciliar document, *Gaudium et Spes*, which spoke of the "genuinely human" also affirmed that "faith throws a new light on all things" (Art 11), especially human works and art.

"By the work of human hands and with the aid of technical means," the earth becomes "a fit dwelling place for all humankind" (Art 57). The same applies to the Church and to churches. "Every effort should be made to encourage" all artists, and "new art forms adapted to our times and in keeping with the characteristics of different nations and regions should be acknowledged by the Church . . . and be brought into the sanctuary whenever they raise the mind to God with suitable forms of expression and in conformity with liturgical requirements" (Art 62).

To be catholic, the church building should reflect an universality of arts and sciences, a careful blending of human talents and artistic works. Reflecting a created and transformed word, the furnishings, vessels, vestments and decor should be a transformed work in and of themselves. Hopefully the day will come, if it is not already here, when the mass-produced will give way to what is fashioned with care, and expressed with sensitivity, and all the arts can find a "home" within the building that houses the Church.

Past and present must also combine, even if new settings are demanded. There is an overriding feeling among many that much was lost or tossed out in the renovation of many of our churches. A truly catholic approach does not overlook what was, but looks at it anew, if only to be sensitive to the feelings of others who found value in it, and a sense of belonging. (By way of example, a rather ornate baptismal font, complete with a towering cover, was found to be no longer serviceable for the rites of baptism; preserved in a wide niche, and altered to be a place of reservation for the Blessed Sacrament, the former font has achieved a new usefulness. For that community, the intimate connection between Baptism and Eucharist has been given an emphasis that might otherwise have been overlooked.)

4. The church should be "apostolic," like the assembly it gathers and sends forth.

A newly-appreciated veneration for the Book of the Scriptures would demand that a separate place within the church be "set aside" for its enthronement. From there the Book may be carried to the place of proclamation, with the solemn procession that has been a tradition within the liturgy. Pehaps that area might provide copies of the Bible to encourage a private and devotional usage when liturgical worship has ended.

But the entire building, as a "sacramental" of the entire Church, should proclaim the gospel of Christ. By its setting and furnishings, the church itself is a tool of evangelization, to members and visitors alike. It recalls the faith that comes from apostles, declares that faith, obliges a recommitment, and holds out the promise of what is yet to come. The altar, by its very shape and size, should say to the onlooker that here a people meets and shares a sacred meal in the presence of their God. The font, with water that can be seen, should speak of cleansing and new life, especially if living plants and ferns support that view. The images of the saints, while recalling the heroes of our faith to memory, should also hold out the promise that ours is a communion of saints, and they are signs of future glory.

By its exterior setting, the building should invite a silent witness that the gospel message is accepted, proclaimed, shared and treasured there. It should also convey a sense that the church is a place from which the community is sent forth into the world, to transform it in the light of faith. It is a place of gathering, a center of worship, and not its totality.

An architect was given a paper to write prior to receiving her degree, and the assignment was to "redesign" the cathedral that had stood in the center of the city for over a century. This was her vision, as she arranged the interior space, since the exterior walls and windows would remain where they always were:

"The cathedral, as a 'seat,' and not merely the place where the bishop sat, relates to the activities of the city itself. From it, as from a central hub, invisible lines radiate outward: as a place where songs are sung to God, the choirspace is on an axis with the symphony hall; as a place where God and humankind sit down to dine, the altar lies on an axis with the newly-renovated market-place, now the focal point of much of the city's energies in renewal; the gospel-shrine is one end of a line that reaches out to the main library nearby; the font, already bearing carvings of ships and sailing, is placed near the one window that overlooks the harbor, with some glass clear enough to enable that the bay be seen. There is room enough for those in love to walk within, and pace without, sensing a love deeper than their own. The various coves, both within and without, shelter the hungry and the homeless, and offer at least a sense of welcome in a world that welcomes them not. In the open galleries, works of art are displayed, and changed, for they express the human emotions that find their enhancement within the worship that is experienced here."

It is a vision that can be added to and expanded, but it is also a truth, and that is the essential task of the house for God's Church — to express, develop, treasure and share what Truth himself has spoken.

Perhaps one can sum up the "marks" of the Church with a characteristic that marks the Church of today — an openness to the world, in which the Church acknowledges oneness with humankind, sees the world as holy, embraces that world in its totality (truly catholic, therefore) and apostolic in seeking to transform it with the gospel message proclaimed and lived. That being so, the church which houses the Church should reflect this "mark." The Church is not a world apart, but a part of the world, and if she gathers together to ponder and celebrate the sacred, it is only because that privilege has been entrusted to her in the vision we call faith.

One senses a sadness that churches remain closed, a solution to the problem of vandalism, one that poses more problems than it seeks to solve. There are no easy solutions, and perhaps it is naiveté that would have us seek to keep our church-houses "open houses." Openness carries risks, but one can hope that such risks be faced, allowing all to enter and discover, in stone and metal, in wood and glass, in cloth and color, the mystery that is the Church.

CHAPTER VIII

MORE THAN FURNISHINGS; SIGNS OF THE SACRED

Every home has its furnishings, and the church-house has its as well, without which the building is an empty space, with nothing to declare. However decorous such furnishings may be, they are more than decorations, and more than simple furniture, although such was their origin and purpose. In point of fact, the individual items within a church took on added meaning with the passage of time, and the deepening awareness of their special use. The sacredness of the Holy Meal lent itself to the very table on which the Food of Life rested, and from which it was distributed. The sacredness of Baptism was expressed by seeing the font itself held in great reverence. Such development is natural to Catholic thought and expression, and if there exists a danger of falling into superstition, the danger also exists of confining such elements to the ordinary and to the practical, thereby robbing creation of its power to transcend itself. Within the necessary tension which both extremes occasion and demand, there is a healthy awareness of the need neither to exaggerate nor underrate.

The furnishings of a church are not mere artifacts, items worth preserving like those on display in a museum. They enable the liturgy to take place, and hopefully to take place with great effect. They have their own role to play, calling attention to what happens when it happens, and to themselves when what happens is over. Thus do they recall, declare, oblige and foresee. Sacred furnishings are practical elements, things to be used, and are also much more than that; they are "sacramentals" intimately related to the worship of God and our communion with one another as Church.

THE ALTAR — Table of the Lord

The earliest Christians tended to avoid the use of the word *altar*, for that word was associated with the place of sacrifice in Jerusalem's temple, and with pagan worship as well. Gathering together in homes to "break the bread," the ordinary table would be used for celebrating the Eucharist, and returned to ordinary usage afterwards. Since the larger homes of those more well-to-do accommodated the communities, the first tables were most likely the three-legged tables found in such homes. It is not difficult to understand that their special usage would lead, in time, to their being used exclusively for sacred purposes, and called "the Lord's table." We find that deacons were in charge of bringing them out for the Eucharist, and responsible for replacing them once the assembly had been dismissed. They were never overly large, therefore, and sometimes quite small, large enough to hold the cup and plate.

By the 4th century, when the basilicas replaced the private homes for worship, the altar began to be fixed to one spot, enabling all to see it, and to gather around it. Other materials began to be used, especially stone, and a deepening awareness of the nature of Christ had its effect upon how such altar/tables were to be considered. The coming together of the various writings of the New Testament facilitated this growth in symbolism.

Jesus Christ was considered "a cornerstone in Zion, an approved stone, and precious" (1 Pt 2:6), and Paul had written that Christians can lay no "foundation other than the one that has been laid, namely Christ Jesus" (1 Cor 3:11). The Book of Revelation, in describing the heavenly worship, depicts Christ as "a Lamb standing, a Lamb that had been slain" (Rev 5:6). The stone altar would become the perfect "visual aid" of such symbolism, and the altar thus began to be viewed as the primary sign of Christ within the church building. In fact, it was seen as the actual cornerstone, the "true cornerstone," of each church. In our day, when steeples are taken as an indication that the building is a church, the origin of the steeple can easily be lost to sight; it was added to the roof of a church or cathedral to indicate the exact position of the altar within the space below.

If Christ could be symbolized by the altar, there was still the concept of the Body of Christ to aid in its further development. With persecutions coming to an end, and with the great reverence that was associated with the martyrs, it was felt that their association with Christ, their death with him, could best be expressed by having their remains (relics) placed within or beneath the altar itself. Revelation depicts "those who had been martyred because of the witness they bore to the word of God" as being "under the altar" (Rv 6:9), and symbolic language soon became stated fact. St. Peter's in Rome sees the High Altar above the chamber where the relics of Simon Peter are said to rest (called the Confessional Altar, after the Latin *confessio*, for the room where martyrs were buried was named after their "confession" of faith in Christ). In time, even to our age, the relics of the martyrs (and other saints) were placed within or beneath the altar itself. With an exaggerated attention to relics, multiplied beyond reason, and resting in elaborate reliquaries, their connection with the altar gradually led to their being placed on top, resulting in having altars turned around, and celebrants facing away from the people.

From that time on, toward the close of the 9th century, the simple "table of the Lord" became a monstrous affair, one that would cause the builders at Babel to blush. Simple relics were replaced with complete statues, often life-sized.

(In one church in downtown Baltimore one may count more figures on the altar than in the congregation.) Often the body of a saint would be encased within the altar, forcing a change from a simple square into an elongated rectangle. Finally, with the reservation of the Blessed Sacrament removed from a separate place and relocated on the altar itself, the evolution of the "table of the Lord" was completed.

There can be no doubt but that the elaborate treatment of the altar coincided with a decline in the reception of the Eucharist. The Mass as something to be viewed, rather than as a meal to be shared, led to the altar as something to be viewed, rather than as the actual table of the Lord where sacrificial Food awaited the participant. With the revision of worship there has come about an appreciation of the altar as the Table of the Lord, where he, the Lamb that was slain, offers himself as food and drink in guise of bread and wine.

A PASTORAL REFLECTION

The rich symbolism of past ages can guide our approach at present. The altar remains the primary symbol of the Lord, and as there is "one Lord," so there should be only one altar. Symbols lose their value when multiplied, and are diminished when expanded. This has always been so, whether it be altars or crosses, and is obvious enough to stand as a principle in its own right. The designation of "side altars" or "other altars" led to *the altar* as Main Altar; the building of new churches, or renovation of existing buildings, should establish that there is one "table of the Lord," just as there is "one cup of blessing" and "one loaf" which we share (1 Cor 10:16,17,21). The altar should be noble in its simplicity, elegant in the beauty of the materials used, large enough to hold the elements for the Eucharist, and uncluttered to allow movement to and from and about it.

The cloth that is used should be brought forth during the preparation of the altar and gifts, not beforehand. Tablecloths indicate that a meal is taking place, otherwise they are simply dust-cloths. And a table is precisely that — a table; it is not a sideboard nor serving cart, and great care should be taken not to make of it a convenient catch-all for non-essentials like vases, missalettes, handkerchiefs or bishop's rings and skullcaps.

There is one lovely custom that may be observed, in order to bring out the significance of the altar. On the day of dedication, or its anniversary, the entire congregation might be invited to come forward in veneration of the altar, as is done by celebrants at the introductory rites. This "rite" is also a possible activity to bring a bible-devotion to its close as well. A prayer is recited, after which all come forward to bow, or to kiss the altar, and then depart; an ancient prayer suggests itself for this purpose:

> "Remain in peace, altar of God, around which the people of God have gathered to offer their very selves in sacrifice.
>
> Remain in peace, altar of God, which bore the weight of mysteries too great for earth alone to bear.
>
> Remain in peace, altar of God, sign of Christ who is our Altar and Victim and Priest.
>
> If we can return here, may it be with deepened hunger for the Sacred Food, and richer hunger for our communion with the Lord and one another.
>
> If we cannot, then may we come before the Heavenly Altar, the Lamb standing as if slain, surrounded by myriads of angels, and saints in solemn assembly. Amen."

THE TABERNACLE — Veiled Presence

For the earliest centuries of the Church's worship, the reservation of the Eucharist was not confined to the church building, and "visits" to the Blessed Sacrament was not a part of one's devotional life. Such reservation was a practical matter, at first, a means of assuring that those absent from the assembly, whether sick or imprisoned, could receive what was truly considered to be "daily bread." There is evidence that members brought home a portion of the consecrated loaf to provide daily fare, both for themselves and members of their household prevented from worshiping with the community.

A simple cabinet sufficed at first, and in time that cabinet was placed within the church building itself, and not in the house of a cleric as previously. In various parts of the world, the reservation of the Eucharist was accomplished by a pillar or tower separate from the altar area, and in Northern France and England a *pyx*, in the form of a dove, was suspended over (or near) the altar. It was during the 16th century that most European churches saw the place of reservation moved to the High Altar, and that practice prevailed down to recent years.

Curious theologies developed, to say the least, as the reception of Holy Communion became a rarity, and the desire to see and venerate the Sacrament of the Altar gained prominence. The ringing of bells, an element of celebration and festivity, soon became signals (to those within and without) as to when the consecration would take place, so the sacred host and chalice might be seen at the moment of elevation.

Yet attention to the reserved Sacrament has always had an important role in Catholic thought and piety, together with the obviously practical matter of providing the Communion to those unable to worship with the entire assembly. The reserved Sacrament will continue to be vital to the one who has partaken, a natural outflowing from Eucharist that is shared, reminder of our communion once the Mass has ended, and continued sign that bread and wine disclose their Creator in veiled form.

A PASTORAL REFLECTION

Practicality dictates that the place of reservation be within easy access of the altar itself, yet distinctly separate, and not hidden from sight, so that members of the community may reflect and ponder, venerate and adore. Secure and locked, the tabernacle should be covered with a veil, for this ancient practice recalls the truth that in the person of Jesus

Christ, God has "pitched his tent" among us. The use of a lamp serves its purpose as well; Samuel slept within "the temple of the Lord" to assure that "the lamp of God" would not be extinguished (1 Sm 3:3), and it was then that he listened to God. There is a rich heritage here, one that reaches into our Jewish ancestry, and one that looks ahead to the day when we are tabernacled in the eternal presence of God, together with all the saints with whom we are in communion.

THE GOSPEL THRONE — Word from the Beginning

In every synagogue the scrolls are preserved and kept within an "ark," from which they are carried in procession, as acclamations are sung, and the people reach out to touch the veils that cover them. As Catholic liturgy developed, this same procession, complete with lights and incense, and in some places a veiled book, was also given its proper place. The Solemn High Mass of our recent past saw the gospel-book carried by subdeacon, accompanied by candle-bearers, and the deacon would chant the gospel facing the people, a remnant of times past before altars were turned to face the wall.

A PASTORAL REFLECTION

Without elaborating on the history of the placement of the gospel-book, which is complex and quite inconclusive, the reverence attending upon the Scriptures would demand a closer look at this important element of worship. The tendency at present is for the lectionary to be carried in procession at the start of Mass, and placed upon the altar until taken up for the liturgy of the Word. This approach has its merits, and indeed something of a history in certain parts of the world, but present need far outweighs presuppositions.

There has been a deepening awareness, within the Catholic Church of the preeminent place of the Scriptures, not only in our public worship but in our private lives as well. As the Eucharist had been accorded a place of reservation within the church, perhaps the need now exists to have the Sacred Scriptures enthroned, so to speak, within their proper place. The practice of the synagogue, and the custom of Protestant churches, suggest this practice in an age of ecumenism, apart from the Catholic Mass, which provides us with the Liturgy of the Word and the Liturgy of the Eucharist in its two-fold structure. John's 6th Chapter, with its double discourse on the Bread of Life (as sustaining word of faith, and as real food and drink), exerts its own influence as well.

On an axis with the pulpit, or *cathedra* of the bishop in cathedral churches, the Gospel-book might be given a place of honor, but without closed cabinet, veil or continuously-burning lamp. From that place it can be brought in procession to the place of proclamation, and returned after homily/creed/intercessions have taken place. Candles that accompany the book could then move to the altar area, and placed near the altar itself as that table is readied for the Eucharistic meal.

There are other possibilities, considering the nature of the Liturgy of the Word itself, although the Gospel-book has traditionally been accorded a prominence of its own. The Bible itself could be used, and brought to the lectern at the beginning of the service of the Word, so that all the readings would make use of the same book. It is a moot question, and one that admits of several approaches, but this much can be admitted: the Word of God demands its proper place in our churches as it does within our worship and our lives, and whatever the resolution, such an honored place should be permanent. Processions at the start and end of our worship pay honor to Christ's presence within the people and the carrying of the Scriptures at these times does little to call attention to that truth.

THE AMBO (PULPIT) — *Word Spoken*

Originally, the ambo or pulpit was a low reading desk, not unlike the platform used for reading the scriptures in synagogues. This lower table allowed the scrolls to be unrolled, and was used only for the reading of the sacred text. In the opening scene of the ministry of Jesus, we find him "standing up to do the reading," and when the book of Isaiah was "handed" to him, "he unrolled the scroll," handing it back to the assistant, and then "sat down" (Lk 4:16-20).

In Christian worship, the readings were read in the same way, and the homily given from the celebrant's chair, for sitting was the correct posture for teaching. Only later do we find sermons being delivered from the place of reading, and this required a higher platform. During the Middle Ages, when the sermon came to take on a life of its own, as it were, did the pulpit begin to move away from the sanctuary, sometimes at quite a distance from it. The pulpit began to be enlarged, or even placed on a supporting pillar, often with something of a "sounding board," rising above it so that the words could be heard, a difficulty in larger cathedrals, needless to say.

Since the bishop's chair was central to the sanctuary area, the pulpit came to be placed somewhere to the right of that chair, and even when the readings took place (read by the celebrant) at an altar no longer facing the congregation, the custom still prevailed, and the book was moved to the "Gospel side" of the altar. This position was seen as appropriate to Christ who is seated at "the right hand of the Father," as the credal formulations assert. Cathedrals proved the exception to the rule, and with the erection of large altars as central to the sanctuary, the bishop's seat was placed to its right; preaching the gospel was the bishop's prerogative, and so the pulpit (for other preachers) came to be moved to the other side, where it is found to this day in cathedrals built before Vatican II.

Quite simply, whether sermons are delivered from pulpit or chair, the pulpit is the place from which the Word of God is publicly read in the hearing of his people. As such, it has a preeminence shared by the altar as a place of activity; this alone would suggest that the Gospel-book not rest on it permanently, nor be enthroned below it, or within it, as is done in some places. (Similarly, the Eucharist is not reserved upon the altar.)

From the simple standpoint of elevation, the proclaimed word should not be done above the entrhoned word; to do so gives the impression that all are not under the imperative of God's Word. There should be one pulpit (lectern) only, given a nobility in structure and material that marks the construction of the altar. If other lecterns are used (cantor, commentator, etc.) they should be portable, not fixed, and not seen as secondary pulpits.

THE FONT — Living Waters

In its celebration of the rites of Baptism, the Church has maintained the tradition of according to this sacrament a place of its own. With the building of churches and basilicas, this separate space often became a separate building, in order to accommodate the large pools into which the candidates would step down, or be immersed. Since the sacrament was seen as *entrance* into the Church, the entrance-way of churches would become the place for the font in many areas. With changing customs, with differing cultures and climates, the font would later become much smaller, and since infant baptism became the norm, a simple basin, elevated to a comfortable height, eventually became standard.

In the light of modern needs, and with the encouragement of the Rite of Christian Initiation of Adults, more attention has been given not only to the size of the font, but to its placement as well. Entry-ways are not out of the question, provided they are ample and comfortable, wide enough to have the assembly gather for baptism, and to enter and leave the building with this "sacramental" of their Christian lives an evident reminder of who they are.

In some churches, the font has been placed within the body of the church itself, symbol of incorporation into the

Body of Christ. In other churches, the font has been given its place within the sanctuary, which seems to draw focus away from the entire inner space as a place of celebration. In building churches, this would appear the less desirable practice.

Whatever the solution, the font should be large enough to accommodate the immersion of infants at least, and provide a clear view of the liturgical action taking place. Readings can take place from the ambo, and all can proceed to the place of baptism; if Easter regains its role as the day of baptism, and immersion is not used, then the font might be of a portable type that can be placed so that all might see. That was not a requirement when separate baptistries were used, and the newly baptized reentered the church proper to be welcomed by the assembly, who had been gathered in song and prayer as the baptisms took place.

In a place of its own, the font can serve as a focal point, especially for those who had been baptized there. Our use of holy water, upon entering the church, had begun as a reminder of this sacrament, and the use of the baptismal font for this purpose would be a welcome use, making of this sacramental a sign that not only recalls, but one that obliges as well, recommitment being a necessary part of our lives in Christ.

THE CHAIR — Presidency among Us

The revision of Catholic liturgy has seen the "presidential chair," the miniature *cathedra* of the presiding bishop, become an essential part of the furnishings. Like the altar itself, this chair had its origins in the ordinary furniture of the houses where the assembly gathered for the Eucharist. The chair used by the head of the household became the seat for the presiding elder, or bishop, and as with the altar, the passing of centuries would witness elaboration, until the final appearance was that of a throne.

It is a chair, and simply that, and celebrants as well as all other members of the community would be uncomfortable with anything resembling a throne. It should have some slight prominence, so that the one who presides can truly preside at the celebration. Nothing would prevent the placement of a microphone nearby, allowing presidential prayers and greetings to take place at the chair, together with the homily, if that seems desirable.

The one who presides among us, leading us in worship, is among us as one who serves, and the chair is the servant's seat, if it is anything at all. Christ holds the primacy in everything; it is he who teaches, he who makes thanksgiving with bread and wine, he who baptizes, and he who is present, in Word and Sacrament, as he is present wherever the Church is gathered in his name. Yet the chair is "sacramental," sign of future glory, as Revelation itself affirms: "I will give the victor the right to sit with me on my throne, as I myself won the victory and took my seat beside my Father on his throne" (Rv 3:21). It is an appropriate symbol as we "have supper with him," and he with us (Rv 3:20).

Neither understated, nor overemphasized, the presidential chair is the seat for the one who presides, and the nature of our liturgy demands that it receive the prominence it deserves. At the same time it should be a sign that all are called to be with the Lord, as indeed the Sacrament of Holy Orders is itself a sign, to the entire Church, of Christ's priestly ministry, and to the world of the redemption he accomplished on its behalf.

A Reconciling Place

The history of the Sacrament of Reconciliation itself reveals the history of the confessional. Once publicly conferred within the sanctuary, this sacrament required a large space where the penitents would lie prostrate, and later be "lifted up" by the right hand of the bishop. Later development saw such space confined to a private area, one in which penitent and confessor could only speak to one another without sight or touch, to play a role in the sacred action. The new rite calls for a separate area, but one which is spacious. It might be a completely open space in larger churches, or a simple room in most buildings. Practicality must have its say in the refurbishing of older churches, so that privacy can be guaranteed, yet ample enough to convey a sense of openness, an openness of space that suggests an openness of mind and heart. Within that space there should be both a kneeler and a chair, so that the penitent may choose either position, and something of a dividing screen to allow for anonymity, if the penitent so chooses. To provide separate confessionals, one with kneeler, and the other with a chair, is unacceptable; it reveals the penitent's choice to others present within the church, and effectively deprives the penitent of that choice when pressed for time.

All too often, one fears, the use of the Bible within the reconciliation area becomes simply ornamental, and the Bible should never be reduced to that. Readings from scripture, a part of the new rite (unfortunately left optional, or confined to the briefest texts), should take place with the use of that book, and not allow the Bible to be a simple furnishing like a lamp or a vase of flowers.

Sacred Images

Perhaps no other element of the church's furnishings has occasioned such hostility and even schism as has the use of icons or statues. The Catholic tradition of employing the arts to portray Christ and his holy ones, and of paying honor to these icons and images, appears to some as a direct violation of God's commandment: "You shall not carve idols for yourselves in the shape of anything . . . you shall not bow down before them or worship them" (Ex 20:4-5). And yet that tradition strongly upholds the words that precede: "You shall not have *other gods* besides me" (Ex 20:3). Our sacred images are not objects of worship, which is given to God alone, but representations of Christ's humanity, and of those human beings who most clearly reflected his presence, for we were created "in the image and likeness of God;" sacred images portray divine images, for such are we as creatures of God.

Within the earliest period of the Church's life, the subject of images was hardly likely to arise. Judaism lived with an abhorrence of idols, and Gentile converts forsook their former ways to follow him who is "the Way." It is only with the rise of Christendom, and the subsequent decline of paganism, that the question ever arose as to the use of art as an expression of faith. The paintings and carvings of the catacombs were to lend their richness to the building of churches, and representations of Christ and his saints became what they have always been — aids to our imagination, focuses of our prayerful thought, and summoners of inner devotedness.

Two separate attitudes toward images have co-existed within the Christian world: the way of images, and the way of the negation of images. Only in times of political upheaval, in which the Church would play a tremendous role, would the issue of "iconoclasm" become a rallying point, as though theology only served to fuel the debate over authority. In the seventh and eighth centuries, political and religious conflicts in the East led to the Second Council of Nicaea which affirmed the usefulness of images to "raise the mind of the spectator to the objects which they represent." At that period, St. John Damascene would correctly discuss the issue within the framework of the sacramental realm, and the role that sensible rites and objects have in the Christian's approach to the sacred.

The debate would emerge again at the time of the Reformation, when images and paintings would be destroyed on a wide scale. Once again the visible arts became the focus of debate concerning authority within the Church, as though the "mistress of the arts" had been exclusively identified with those arts.

Historians of art see these epochs as an instinct, supported by religious motivation, to destroy anything comely and beautiful. A break with the past all too often involves actual breakage, whether concerning the 365 crosses of the island of Iona which were cast into the sea at the time of the Reformation, or the tea tossed overboard into Boston's harbor at the time of the American Revolution. When reason is overshadowed by emotion, the past, it seems, must give way to the future, and the very destruction of images becomes symbolic of an inner approach.

In all honesty, and with consideration for a different approach to religious value, iconoclasm could be seen as an attempt to purify religion, and force a return to essentials. To assert the primacy of God, appeal was made to the commandment given on Sinai; to assert the primacy of Scripture, all that was not scriptural was cast aside.

Yet within the Church's reaction to these upheavals the primacy of God and his sacred Word are not denied. The retention of statues and ritual provided a means whereby ordinary people could satisfy their deepest impulses, so that their minds and hearts could be at peace. The monumental proportions of the statues carved during the Catholic Revival were a means of asserting this truth. The statues were cast in heroic dimensions to reveal that passionate concern for sanctity that marked the lives of those whom the Church declared to be saints of God. Such statues are in and of themselves an answer to those who would destroy the role of art within the Catholic tradition.

One is reminded of Aeneas, whose journey of seven years was recorded by Virgil in the *Aeneid*. Tossed about upon the sea, he comes to a land where barbarous peoples were thought to live, and he is overcome with fear, until he views their artful carvings and bas-reliefs. "These people know the pathos of life," he declares, "and mortal things can touch their hearts." With that his fear subsided as certainly as did the storm that found him shipwrecked there.

Images express faith in a way that words cannot, and *vice versa*. Moreover they express the artist's faith, just as any work of art does not simply convey an object, but the naming of that object. One cannot look at the history of art without sensing that the power of art to move is derived from the power of the artist and the viewer to be moved. Art became abstract, one could say, when photography began to emerge to "capture" reality. Photographs of modern saints are curious things at best; rarely do they capture the very soul of the person whose soul was moved by grace.

The denial of statues and paintings, whether of Christ or his saints, is (for the Catholic tradition, at least) a failure of the "genuinely human" to "find its echo in our hearts." A representation of a woman and child is not a figure of the Madonna, despite a similarity of pose. Actual photographs of Abraham Lincoln convey none of the power that the statue in his memorial at Washington does.

As sacramentals, sacred images are precisely that — sacred. They are *signs that recall* that women and men have responded to God's call throughout history; carvings, like legends and myths, enlarge the actual person, in much the same way that grace enlarged their lives, and in precisely the same way that Jesus is not simply "the carpenter's son" (Mt 13:55). They are *signs that oblige* us to respond to the call to be holy as God is holy. They are, thereby, reminders of our failure, and shame us as we confront our own response to the gospel of Christ. Further, they are *signs that foresee*, looking to the day when we, too, will be with the Lord. Placed upon pillars, they can be signs of the scriptural truth: "I will make the victor a pillar in the temple of my God ... the new Jerusalem" (Rv 3:12).

Their placement, however, should never be merely ornamental; such images are far too important for that. Nor should they intrude upon the focal points of our liturgy; it is too important to allow such intrusion. The images of the saints, which recall our communion with them, is a secondary item within the liturgical space, and their importance should be neither ignored nor exaggerated.

The Catholic Church has always maintained the rightness of images and icons to exist in her "homes" as in the homes of her faithful. They declare the truth of the Incarnation, and allow the "genuinely human" to declare this truth as well. Music embodies the word, especially the psalms, and architecture lifts spire heavenwards like litanies; sculpture and painting can do no less as their artistry is transformed into ministry.

God became a human being; were that even to have taken place in an age of photography, the question of images might never have arisen. Since the mind must ponder his appearance, then the mind seeks aids to thought as it does in every other sphere of activity. The Lord, the Virgin who bore him, and the holy women and men who bore likeness to him by grace, are all the subject of the artist's theme, as they are the subject of our own prayers and praise.

Stations of the Cross

As we are called to take up our cross as followers of Christ, the "stations" serve to reinforce that truth. They are also a sign that we are a pilgrim people, and such movement, whether in private or in common, is a valued expression of that simple truth. The actual "station" has always been the simple cross, but representations of the scenes have become the acceptable and common practice. As with the images of saints, the "stations" should be of such a size and design as to acquire their proper prominence when in use, and recede into the background during the liturgical services.

Incense

This object, considered so much a part of our Catholic tradition, can be viewed as a sacramental that is most readily associated with the concept of the church as sacred space. The Hebrew Scriptures record a detailed ceremony for the making of incense (Ex 30:34-38, for example), and frankincense was one of the gifts that astrologers are shown bringing to the newborn son of Mary (Mt 2:11).

Its use in Christian worship seems to have been drawn from its appearance in Revelation, as "the smoke of the incense went up before God, and with it the prayers of God's people" (Rv 8:4). Used in ancient times by the Emperor, a sign of special honor, it was "borrowed" by the Church, originally as a mark of respect for the pope, and then extended to all bishops. From thence it became a mark of respect for sacred objects, such as the altar or Gospel-book.

It has its own value, even if our modern approach cannot

associate it with "the prayers of God's people." It is Paul who provides an excellent symbolism for this simple element of earth:

> "Thanks be to God who unfailingly leads us on in Christ's triumphal train, and employs us to diffuse the fragrance of his knowledge everywhere! We are an aroma (incense) of Christ for God's sake" (2 Cor:14).

Thus, the Word of God validates the use of this sacramental, a sign of what the Christian is called to be — an element of earth that leads others to consider Christ.

Lights

Apart from the Paschal Candle, the Church has also made use of lamps and other candles in her long history. These "natural" forms of illumination were a necessity in the earliest days of her worship, and the custom of "blessing" the evening lights took a public form in the liturgical hour of vespers or Evening Praise.

They are more than simple necessities, however, and came to be seen as symbolic, not only of Christ and his Resurrection, but also of his sacrifice. Originally, altar candles were the torches that preceded the pope as he entered the basilicas of Rome, an honor accorded the Bishop of Rome by the emperors. Once he had arrived at the altar, the candles were arranged around the altar, or preceded the Gospel-book, and the practice became universal.

Their placement near the altar led to their being seen as symbolic of the sacrificial death of Jesus. The melting wax (or oil, in hanging lamps) was taken to represent the gift of self on behalf of others, such as Jesus made upon the cross, and the martyrs in their own deaths. The candles, or lamps, that burned near the altar and over the tombs of the martyrs soon became "votive" candles, sign of one's own gift of self, especially for those unable to "spend time" in prayer. Their use continues, and is encouraged, sacramental of ourselves as givers of self, and light to others.

CHAPTER IX

THE ELEMENTS OF WORSHIP

Apart from the "furnishings," themselves sacramentals of who we are as members of God's household, there are other elements associated with the church that houses the Church. These are the elements of worship, born of our shared human experience (clothing, vessels, gestures and movement), and important to salvation's history (the worship of Israel and New Testament worship) which have acquired added meaning. Such elements *recall* that history, *declare* our own understanding of the Church and the Sacraments, *oblige* us to live out the meaning of faith, and *foresee* the eternal worship in which eternal life has been viewed.

SACRED VESTMENTS
"Put on the Lord Jesus Christ"
(Rom 13:14)

If any of us belong to that group which refuses to be "trendy," and insists on wearing last year's styles, we are in good company. The vestments that have become traditional within our liturgy are simply the ordinary clothing of yesteryear. They are the style of ancient Rome, the garb of the ordinary citizen at an age when the Church assumed its position of prominence within the world.

Whatever rank or status the average Roman citizen held, whether senator or tradesman, each wore two basic garments, an inner robe and an outer cloak. The undergarment was a long robe, which reached to the ankles, and was kept in place by a cord, or cincture, that was easily knotted; the color was white, as a rule, and the material fairly light in texture. As for the outer garment, it was a long cloak that covered the body on all sides, and had a hood for inclement weather, much like the *poncho* worn in South America, or by American Marines. It was called a *pluviale* (from *pluvium*, the Latin word for "rain"), the name still given to the cope worn in processions, etc.

Underwear and raincoats. It's as simple as that.

During the 5th and 6th centuries, that saw the barbarian invasions, ordinary clothing began to change in style, and shorter robes became the order of the day, except in the churches. Accustomed to wearing their "Sunday best" at the altar, the clergy continued to wear the older form of garments, including what we would call "accessories" (the scarf, which would become the bishop's *pallium*, and the long handkerchiefs, tied about the wrist, known as *maniples*, dropped from liturgical usage in the present century). Society went its way, modernizing its dress, and the clergy went their way, providing us with the concept of vestments, most of them still in use.

The Amice

A late intrusion into the liturgy, this simple square cloth was worn by monks to protect the neck and throat and had strings attached, so that it served as an apron for work. Worn by priests during the Middle Ages, as they came and went to the altar, it became bothersome to tie and untie, and so "sneaked into" the classification of vestments. Since it covered the head while the other vestments were put on, it received the rather dubious symbolism of "the helmet of salvation" (Eph 6:17).

The Alb

To put it quite simply, this is the undergarment of ancient Rome, and its whiteness led it to become the baptismal robe in early rites of initiation. "Who are these people all dressed in white?" (Rev 7:13), the seer asked, and the newly baptized could answer, "We are!" Long associated in scripture with the "new age," the white robes (*alba* means "white" in Latin) gained a baptismal significance. Later, in the course of time, that color came to signify purity and innocence, as in the wedding gowns of our own day. Accordingly, the robe served to recall the clergy to their commitment of celibacy once that discipline became standardized, and finally mandatory.

The Cincture

This cord did for the average citizen of Rome what the belt does in today's world; it simply keeps things in place. From a purely practical matter, the cincture, which is knotted in the middle allowing both ends to dangle, was viewed as a symbol of chastity. If the symbolic mind went to work and saw significance in everything, at least it was not without a sense of humor!

The Chasuble

The Latin *casula* ("little house") gives us our chasuble, the vestment that has traditionally been associated with the celebration of the Eucharist. It resembled the raincoat, but was not intended for inclement weather, and so was without a hood. Like the *pluviale*, however, it did cover the entire body on all sides, that is until the scissors were taken out and used. It was an ample vestment well into the 16th century, but the use of heavier materials, including damask and brocade, led to a change in style; the sides were snipped away to allow for arm movement, and well into this century the chasuble resembled a sandwich-board more than an ample and flowing garment.

They became a place for "advertisements," so to speak, decorated with symbols and pictures of the Lord and his saints. Because its symbolism was lost, it was felt necessary to adorn it with symbols, as is still the custom, unfortunately. (With Mass facing the people, chasubles started appearing with symbols on the front, so as not to deprive the people of a conflicting confusion of symbols to which religious goods dealers had accustomed us.)

The basic symbolism is one of "love," according to the author of Colossians, who asks his readers to "clothe" themselves with virtues, and "over all these virtues put on love" (Col 3:12,13), that same love which "covers a multitude of sins" (1 Pt 4:8).

The Stole

Wearing a towel around one's neck is an acceptable custom for swimmers and bathers, and was a common practice in ancient Rome. Soon, however, this towel became a mark of distinction, and even a sign of one's official status. It was a long, narrow strip of cloth, and in time its color became a mark of public office and authority; as such it entered the Church's liturgy, although it, too, had a practical use. It served the function of a modern-day scarf, protecting the neck in winter, and an absorbent towel in hot weather.

One doubts that this was so, for its use as a mark of rank would easily have made it welcome at a time when distinctions between laity and clergy were beginning to be made. The deacon's stole, worn over one shoulder, did arise from practicality; worn over the shoulder, it served as a napkin for serving people at the *agape* supper, and at the Eucharist as well. Originally long and narrow, and reaching to the feet, later centuries would see the scissors at work again, until late centuries saw it sadly shortened, its ends broadened until they resembled shovels.

As a symbol, the stole came to be seen as the "robe of innocence" which had been lost by the fall of Eve and Adam in Eden. Considering what happened to its design over the course of centuries, one can only appreciate that symbolism all the more! Whatever its symbolism, however, it remained a mark of rank and authority, worn by those in Holy Orders.

The Dalmatic.

Deacons may be surprised to learn that their distinctive outer garment takes its name from the tunic that was worn by ordinary peasants in Dalmatia. Its use as a vestment began in Rome, where the pope wore this garment under his chasuble, and bestowed the privilege of having it worn by deacons in the 4th century. Later conceded to bishops elsewhere, it was worn by deacons and priests everywhere. Until the present, the bishop wore the tunic (the garb of sub-deacons) and the dalmatic under his chasuble, to show that he held the fullness of priestly power, which probably explains why pontifical Masses started so late.

As a sleeved garment, it is the proper robe of the deacon, and a liturgical vestment. It should reach at least to a point just above the alb, and like all vestments, be attractive, ample and flowing, allowing grace of movement, and the full display of color, texture and warmth.

From ordinary usage, other garments entered the service of the liturgy, including caps, or hats. The simple skullcap, worn to protect the head in cold weather, would acquire a small knot to make it easier to take off (later, a pom-pom), and emerge as the *biretta*, now fairly discarded. The *mitre* worn by popes and bishops began to be used only in the 9th century, but has persisted to this day as an insignia of office; the simple pastoral staff, a plain stick with a crossstick at the top, and called a *crozier* because of its resemblance to the cross, would become a shepherd's crook, after its general introduction in the same century. (The present popes, since Paul VI, have returned to the cross-shaped staff, which is an extraordinarily beautiful symbol.)

Gloves and shoes, rings and crosses, all borrowed from ordinary use, would enter the liturgy and become marks of rank, or insignia. The very practical *surplice* (from *super pellicum*, a garment worn "over the skins") used for warmth as monks sang the nighttime hours, would become the vestment favored by those no longer con-celebrating, as well as by those preaching. The history of each vestment, marked by practicality and not a little humor, still points to a tradition that has been found worthy of keeping. Vestments convey a sense of timelessness, and add grace and beauty (as long as they are graceful and beautiful, elegant in their style and simplicity, and left unadorned by a multitude of symbols). They *recall* the worship of Israel and the Church; they *declare* that we have "put on Christ," and are new creation in him; they *oblige* us to consider that our outer selves must convey inner attitudes; and they *foresee* the day when all humankind will be clothed in dignity, not only in the glory that awaits, but even upon the earth, which is being transformed by grace. They are grace-full signs, with hues and colors that add festivity to our celebrations before God, just as color marks our own festivities in life.

SACRED VESSELS
"This Treasure We Possess" (2 Cor 4:7)

Once again the practical has become the symbolic. Bread and wine, whether served at home, or served within the Eucharist where they are no longer simple bread and wine, demands a plate and cup. Oil for anointings requires a vessel, as does water for baptism and sprinkling. The same development that saw the ordinary table become the Lord's table, and set aside for that use alone, would see plate and cup and bowl similarly take on special and reserved usage, and symbolic meaning as well.

The Cup

The *chalice* (from the Latin *calix*, for "cup") is simply that — a cup. Originally, the ordinary vessels for meals were used, and stone and wood provided the basic materials. The use of "one cup" saw the earliest chalices with handles on either side, and from about the 4th century, metals, especially precious metals, would be used. They varied in size and shape, some of them simple goblets, others approaching the dimensions of a vase. Many were adorned with gems, and as the desire for elegance became the overriding concern, the chalice became taller, and elaborately decorated; with communion under both forms gradually disappearing, the actual cup would become smaller, with some of them capable of holding no more than a few tablespoons of wine.

From simple vessels, chalices were to become works of art, and artistic restraint was itself restrained, as angels, baskets of fruit, and even mermaids began to decorate them. It was not until the present century that any attention was paid to recovering a sense of simplicity and quiet beauty. With the return of the cup to the laity, a return to the practical became a necessity, and the use of a decanter (to maintain the symbolism of "one cup," over the use of several cups) made its return as well.

The Plate

We call it a *paten*, and have come to think of this vessel for bread as a small, flat disk, sufficient for one large host. The very name suggests otherwise, for *patena* is the Latin word for "platter." It was necessary, when introduced from the start of Christian worship, to have the many large breads placed upon one dish. The notion of "one bread," it seems, lies more in the fact that such small loaves were one *type* of bread; the earliest representations for the Eucharist show several small loaves, recalling the multiplication of loaves and fishes.

The history of the plate closely follows that of the cup, large at first, and increasingly smaller in size as communion became a rare event.

The chalice and paten are the basic vessels, and others are derived from them. The *ciborium* is a cup, fitted with a lid, and used to reserve the Holy Sacrament. The *monstrance* (from *monstra*, the Latin for "show") was introduced when devotion to the Blessed Sacrament increased, concomitant to a decrease in the reception of the Eucharistic Food. The *oil-stock* began as a vessel for the holy oils (Chrism, Oil of the Sick, and Oil of Catechumens) and decreased in size out of practical purposes.

All are vessels, and as such, are seen as sacramentals, not because they contain the sacred elements of our worship, but because they point out that we are vessels. "God . . . has shone in our hearts," St. Paul writes; "this treasure we possess in earthen vessels, to make it clear that its surpassing power comes from God and not from us" (2 Cor 4:6,7). Sacred vessels, therefore, should resemble us somehow — carefully created, coming from the earth, capable of holding and being held, and treasured. In their simplicity and simple nobility, they should speak to us of how we are to treasure one another, vessels of God's presence in the world.

GESTURE AND MOVEMENT
"with blameless hands held aloft" (1 Tm 2:8)

Jesus Christ is that "life become visible" which his disciples "have heard ... seen ... looked upon ... and touched" (1 Jn 1:1,2). Our lives, as modern followers, are no less a tribute to the power of the senses to see and hear and look upon and even touch the same Lord whom first disciples accompanied. Movement and touch are ways in which we communicate our feelings and innermost thoughts, not only to others, but to ourselves as well. The world of the sacred is not a world of its own; dance and marches, applause and lowered heads, these all speak in ways profane and sacred, and are as common to the workaday world as to that sacred work we call liturgy.

When words fail, as they so often do, there must be another way to communicate what we are and how we feel. For the speech-impaired, hands form a language of their own; we call it "sign-language," and the hyphen is a statement in itself. Even when our speech is not impaired, hands accompany lips to make the message clear. Public speakers rarely fail to use their eyes or hands as they talk, for words alone seem naked somehow when not accompanied by the body's own language.

Among the parts of the body used to communicate, hands seem to have a preeminence. Even among those for whom images and statues have no place within religious expression, the famous "praying hands" of Albrecht Durer seem to hold a favored place. For us within the Catholic tradition, no other gesture has such power to express our faith in the redemptive mystery than hands that make the *sign* of the cross. Whether formed by a celebrant in blessing, or by any member of the community in so many circumstances (entering a church, thus recalling our baptism into the "name" of Father, Son and Spirit; before any prayer; at mealtime, etc.), the sign of the cross has become an identifying mark for Catholic Christians.

We *sing* the cross's power, and we *sign* its triumph over us. We declare that mind must fathom its mystery, heart must embrace its effectiveness, and shoulders must be willing to take up our own cross in imitation of the Lord. We measure the universe, bringing it within confined and personal perview, as though to say we "grasp fully, with all the holy ones, the breadth and length and height and depth of Christ's love" (Eph 3:18).

Within the history of the celebration of the Eucharist, the tradition of hands "held aloft" continued its long history from the Jewish practice of prayer, whether in private or in public. As the course of that liturgical history developed, the gesture, once common to all participants, became a rubric for the celebrants alone. It was to be so regularized as to become uncomfortable, with celebrant required to hold his hands no higher than his shoulders, and no wider as well. Even the uncomfortableness acquired a meaning of its own, a symbol of suffering and sacrifice (thankfully denied to all present, one feels).

But other gestures and movement acquired deeper meaning as well. Participation was never confined to merely standing by, or simply sitting, as though passivity (itself symbolic) were the sole measurement of activity. We walk to church, and should walk within as well. Processions are sacramentals to our pilgrim minds, the sacred form of marches and parades which children of all cultures seem to form. If bowing is not a part of our culture, it is common to most cultures, and even Western traditions associate the nodding of the head as a form of recognition and respect.

We lift up our hands to declare that we "lift up" our heart, as the beginning of our Eucharistic Prayers demand us to do. Extended hands are precisely that, movement that goes outward, taking us beyond ourselves. We genuflect, even if the knee fails to touch the floor, for it is a way of saying what Paul declared: "at Jesus' name every knee must bend" (Phil 2:10). We have the beautiful custom of bowing our heads whenever his sacred name is uttered; it is our way of saying, once again with Paul, that Jesus Christ was "never anything but 'yes' to God" (1 Cor 1:19). That nod reflects the moment of his death, the moment of his "yes" to the Father's will. Among some Catholics, the nodding of the head is done during the Lord's Prayer, when one affirms Christ's request that the Father's will "be done."

Such movements, however slight, are no less significant thereby. They claim their own right to speak, and should never be silenced. It was embarrassment that led the "kiss of peace" to determine a new meaning for the Sacrament of Confirmation. The presiding bishop would touch fingers to lips, and then touch the cheek of the one being confirmed; gone was the actual "kiss," but not the notion of "peace," for the bishop still said "Peace be with you." If anyone doubts the power of gesture to speak more loudly than words, Confirmation provided the most noticeable example. The actual words were overlooked, and the gesture of hand to cheek said something new — a tap to remind the confirmed one that she or he must be willing to suffer for the cause of Christ! That became the prevailing sign, the dominant theme, within this sacrament, and guided the Church's own perception of her rite. One was no longer simply confirmed, and one's initiation taken to its second step; instead, the baptized was given a new role, that of "soldier" for Christ.

For many there will always be an uncomfortableness with gestures; most likely it reflects an inability to be comfortable with ourselves, or at the least an inability to sense what is truly appropriate within a sacred place. David, dancing before the ark, brought cheers and applause and even more dancing to the crowds who lined his path. He would have a hard time of it dancing up our aisles! We would rather confine his movements, one might say, and keep him safely within a window near the choir loft, holding his harp, but not playing it!

For many, the world of movement seems a strange world

within the realm of the sacred, even though it is second nature to our Catholic approach to life, with genuflections, kneeling, standing, and the like. One can only remember the recent past with some tinge of humor, especially when recalling how those who were not Catholic felt reluctant to attend Mass simply because the ritual movement within the pews seemed so complicated, let alone that ritual movement that took place within the sanctuary. Only when we understand that the whole person engages in worship will we feel free to allow movement itself to represent our approach, our drawing near to God.

But such gestures do fall within the realm of sacramentals. They have their counterpart within the rest of the world. We stand as a mark of honor or respect; we kneel instinctively for prayer in our own rooms; we walk together to show that we are together, as though pilgrimage were a way of life; we fold our hands as token of things held and held dear; we move them outward in exuberance or elation; we sit as listeners. Most importantly, we touch one another, members of the same Body, even as we reach out to receive the eucharistic Body.

Nothing "genuinely human" should fail to find its "echo" within the heart of those who worship, for it is we who worship, and not merely part of us.

AN EPILOGUE TO PART THREE

AN ETERNAL DWELLING

There is one sacred space that is often overlooked as such. That is the sacred ground known as the cemetery. Christian art was born there, within the burial places of ancient times, especially in the catacombs of Rome. Places of death were customarily adorned to speak about life, and for Christians, those places were to speak about eternal life, adorned with representations of the Eucharist, or with a glorious image of the one who died for us, conveyed by a glorious and triumphant cross.

The earliest cemeteries allowed the well-to-do to build large tombs, ones that could accommodate entire families for a meal. That very notion would enable the Christians to enlarge their own view of family, allowing sisters and brothers in Christ to gather there and express their faith (although the notion of celebrating the Eucharist there is largely a myth). The "borrowed" tomb of Joseph of Arimathea lent the gospel's authority to such gatherings, which took on the aspect of not merely commemorating the dead, but of celebrating their triumph over death.

When the remains of the martyrs, honored by members of the community, were allowed to be transferred to public churches, the custom soon arose of having the faithful buried within the same building, or at least in an undercroft.

This was especially true of the clergy, a fitting gesture of respect for those who had presided at worship there. As a matter of sheer necessity, the area around the churches became the place for burial, and were viewed as an extension of the church, therefore as sacred ground.

Even if no longer close to the church building, cemeteries have never lost their significance as holy ground. It is a place of hope enlightened by faith, as indeed all the earth speaks of such hope, however faintly such sounds are perceived. A natural reverence overtakes anyone entering a cemetery, a holy fear, not a fear motivated by dread or fright. Any vandalism produces only shock and revulsion; we feel that we are violated, and not merely the area itself.

Funeral customs may change, and cremation may become the commonplace, but a special place for those who "died in the Lord" will remain a part of our heritage. Hopefully the day is over when one spoke of "unconsecrated" ground, the separate place for sinners or those denied the "right" of Christian burial. Sinners have every right to be there, where the ground is holy, as they do within the sacred space we call a church. Holy ground is the proper place for sinners to be, which is why we must feel so welcome in church.

The tradition has been to mark the cemetery with a cross or crucifix, large enough for all to see. Cemeteries, no less than the cross itself, are signs of life, not of death, and the crucifix is rightly placed within them as within the sanctuary.

PART FOUR

THE SACREDNESS OF PERSONS AND THINGS

The creation would have remained incomplete without "the sixth day," when the earth brought forth "all kinds of living creatures," and God created "male and female" in "his own image" (Gn 1:24,27). As some read the story, the "fall" seems to provide a sad and inevitable conclusion to that day, but the first chapters of Genesis represent the beginning of the story, and not its ending.

Within the words of banishment spoken to "our firt parents," and to the serpent who deceived them, there are faint traces of an outcome that is still being realized. The author of Ephesians looked upon the whole story, and traced within it "the mysterious design which for ages was hidden in God" (Eph 3:9). He saw what the earliest Christian writers saw — a *proto-evangelium*, a glimmer of gospel, a first revelation of good news, and a hint of the eventual outcome.

There would be "enmity" between the woman's "offspring" and that of "the serpent" (Gn 3:15). But continuity, and not destruction, would mark the course of that enmity. It has been so from start to present, and will be so from present to finish. Tucked within the tale of banishment and exile one finds a small "sacramental," so to speak. Adam and Eve had sewn "fig leaves" together and "made loin-cloths for themselves" as they "hid themselves from the Lord" (Gn 3:7,8). Yet, once the words of exile had been pronounced, a sentence of doom, we find that "the Lord God made leather garments with which he clothed them" (Gn 3:21). Within a seemingly insignificant gesture there lies an echo of the "hidden design" of which Ephesians speaks. The Lord had fixed purpose in mind; his creation would not be undone.

As salvation's history continued, other "sacramentals" would make their appearance. The role of garments, to take but one example, would continue, as God's people were commissioned to "put tassels on the corner of their garments." It was to be a "sign" to "remind" them "to keep all the commandments of God without going wantonly astray" (Nm 15:37-41). A further means of enshrining the commandments (*words*, in Hebrew) would be the phylacteries which the Israelites were to "bind at the wrist as a *sign*," and as "a pendant on the forehead" (Dt 6:8). The *word* of God would also be affixed "on the doorposts" of houses and gates," a custom that continues in the *mezuzah* found at the entrance to Jewish homes of today.

If time and place served to remind one of God's grace, persons and things would play no less a role. It could not be otherwise in a world peopled with "images of God" that were of his own making. The word that summoned Woman and Man into being would summon Abraham to leave his native land, and command Moses to draw near his presence on Sinai. Patriarchs, prophets, priests and parents, kings and servants — all would be summoned before the Lord, each with God's appointed task.

The God who spoke in "fragmentary ways" would finally speak through another person — "his Son" (Heb 1:1). As Matthew begins the story of "Jesus Christ, son of David, son of Abraham" (Mt 1:1), he would trace an ancestry of persons — Judah and Rahab and Ruth and David, and finally Joseph and Mary. The author of Hebrews would delineate that "ancestry" further, as he summons into view "a cloud of witnesses" (Hb 12:1). The procession continues into the present, swelled by ranks of martyrs and confessors, and holy women and men of every age. It is a living litany of saints *and* sinners, a litany of persons called to holiness, and sacred therefore.

Were we to summon them before our mind's eyes, we would see what artists have seen for centuries, for they would not appear before us empty-handed. Ruth would be bearing her sheaves, and David his harp or slingshot, for he was adept at the use of both. Melchizedek would still be carrying the bread and wine he brought out to Abraham; he does it still whenever the first Eucharistic Prayer is offered. Laurence would carry his grill and martyr's palm, an uncomfortable thought for all Laurences, and Kateri Tekakwitha would wear her Indian shawl, and firmly cling to the small cross she had fashioned from twigs.

Persons and the things they use, no less than time and space, speak to us of a creation that reaches toward its fulfillment, towards the completion of a design no longer hidden. Remaining what they are (*persons* bearing resemblance to God, and *things* that bear the deeper stamp of God's own tooling), they attain a deeper meaning. Persons and things are God's own servants, and both are sacramentals. They declare that nothing is without value, and that nobody is insignificant.

Those who would affirm the priority of the scriptures (word) by denying the rightful place of sacramentals (deeds) fail to appreciate that most of the scriptures are written in couplets. Our tradition affirms, in harmony with the Psalmist, that "the Lord is faithful in all his *words* and holy in all his *works* (Ps 145:13).

With Sirach we affirm that "the works of God are *all of them* good" and there is "no cause to say: 'This is not as good as that'; for each shows forth its worth at the proper time" (Sir 39:33-34).

The "proper time" is that moment when the Church performs her Rites of Blessing. We find that persons and things are blessings and must lead us to bless the God who sustains the creation his hands have formed.

And so we look at the *Ritual* itself which upholds the

truth which Holy Scripture records: "Everything in heaven
and on earth was created" in Christ, "and it has pleased God
by means of him to reconcile *everything* in his *person*, both
on earth and in heaven" (Col 1:16, 19-20).

CHAPTER X

BLESSINGS

Since the days of Vatican II, Catholics accustomed to a liturgy which seemed changeless (and eternally timeless, therefore) have witnessed a revision of rites. Our ways of worship have changed, and so have we in the process. Renewal is seen as properly belonging to the "how" as well as the "who" of liturgical expressions of faith. Scriptures have regained their rightful place of prominence, vernacular languages their primacy in communicating thoughts and ideas, and active participation its preeminent role in the non-verbal language that is ours by the very nature of things.

For some the changes represent a *terminus ad quem*, a goal that has been reached; for others they are a *terminus a quo*, a starting-point. There is truth inherent in both perspectives, but the latter view has nature and history on its side. It is in the very nature of things that growth accompany life, and our worship is a living thing. The reign of God demands such growth, else the "mustard seed" could have been replaced by a grain of sand, equally small, yet unchanging. Such was not the case. The Lord chose well and wisely to select the seed to be a parable.

If sacramentals have been viewed, in the past, as matters of little consequence, the revision of the *Ritual* is not without significance. It has an impact and importance that the apparently insignificant often bears. Like the mustard seed, the *Book of Blessings* speaks to us of a kingdom's growth. Like the sacramentals it organizes and develops, the new *Ritual* addresses itself to the people of God in their understanding of self, and their appreciation of the world in which they live, and of which they are a part.

"Whatever came to be in him," the Word that "became flesh," is seen to have found "life" (Jn 1:3,14). That is the truth which forms the beam and hasp of things from which hang the rites of blessing, and the sacramentals. Our "blessings" invite "all on earth" to "come and see the works of God" (Ps 66:5). It recalls the Church to declare aloud: "Bless the Lord, O my soul, and forget not all his benefits" (Ps 103:2). All that is declares itself to be a blessing, and moves us to bless the God whose provident love is revealed in all that he carefully fashioned, and which he continues to fashion anew.

"Praised be the God and Father of our Lord Jesus Christ, who has bestowed on us in Christ every spiritual blessing" (Eph 1:3). That is the very text which sacramentals teach, and for which they form a commentary. The realities of earth are summoned before the Church, in much the same way that creation was brought before Adam, and receives a new name. Each is henceforth known as "blessed," or "a blessing." Earth speaks of heaven, in these rites, openly revealing the imprint of the creator's hand.

Matthew's Gospel portrays Jesus as blessing God, and offering "praise" for what lies "hidden" (Mt 11:25). He continues to do so from within his Church, which discloses the hidden meaning of all that is. It is no different a praising of the Father's wisdom for the revelation of his Christ. It is done in the same way as the Savior could declare "blessed" those who are "poor in spirit . . . sorrowing . . . the single-hearted . . . the peacemakers . . . and those who suffer persecution" (Mt 5:3-12). Such as these had never been called "blessed" before, and even if the world itself rejects the term, such they are, and such they will remain. As with persons, so with things. Both are declared to be blessed and blessing both, and the word that declares it to be so is the very Word by which all things were made.

Finding the gift of the Son to be a "blessing," and utter proof that "God so loved the world" (Jn 3:16), the Church acknowledges the receipt of the Spirit as gift and blessing. Moved by that Spirit, she works in service to the world, sharing blessings, and deepening the perception of values. "The people of God believes that it is led by the Spirit of God who fills the *whole* world. Moved by that faith it tries to discern in the event, the needs, and the longings it shares with others of our time, what may be genuine *signs* of the presence or purpose of God ... the mission of the Church will show itself to be supremely human by the very fact of being religious" (*Gaudium et Spes*, Art 11).

This is the guiding principle behind the revision of the *Book of Blessings*. It is a revision, if you will, of the Church's understanding of the world of which it is a part, and the vision guides the Church as it moves from end to beginning. Moving from begining to end would only disclose the ways of the world without that reversal of things, that active renewal of vigor "like the eagle's," which is the Spirit's presence.

The Book of Blessings

Within the various chapters that comprise the *Book of Blessings*, one can detect a priority of values that flow from the spirit and teachings of the Second Vatican Council. In its encouragement of different nations and regions to study and suggest additional rites, that wider view of the Church is already at work; in its catholicity of purpose and outlook, the *Book of Blessings* truly looks at the entire creation, and sees it as continuing. Neither creation itself, nor the blessings that declare creation's God, is a finished work; the present revision is precisely that, a revision for the present. It allows the past to continue in force, and guides the future. The rites of blessing would see the Church herself as a "scribe," by her writings, one "learned in the reign of God," able to bring forth from the "storeroom" of its tradition "both the old and the new" (Mt 13:52).

The *Book of Blessings* divides itself into five parts.

Part One: Blessings Related to Persons

The blessing of "families," together with a yearly blessing in their homes, comes first, followed by rites which invoke God's blessing upon children, engaged couples, mothers before or after the birth of a child, and the elderly who are confined.

The sanctification of the home has been a special concern, especially in recent years. It would only be natural for the Church, which considers itself to be God's family, to encourage the view of the family as an *ecclesia domestica*, a portion of the Church within the home, a gathering of the Church according to the promise of Christ, "Where two or three are gathered in my name, there I am in their midst" (Mt 18:20). Future revisions will see this concept widen, especially since single persons have often been viewed by society in general as somehow apart from their center, as though there existed no such thing as a vocation to be single.

The rites that follow those for persons at home ask blessings upon the sick, those sent to preach the Gospel, study and prayer groups, organizations dedicated to public safety, pilgrims and travelers.

Part Two: Blessings Related to the Faithful, their Buildings and Activities

These rites continue the priority that has been placed upon persons within the Church: their homes, new buildings, seminaries and schools, libraries and offices, together with public buildings (hospitals, etc.) The blessing of facilities for communication, technical equipment, athletic fields or gymnasia, and the blessings for animals, fields, livestock, harvests and meals are also included. In a word, the entire sphere of human activity, or as *Gaudium et Spes* put it, everything "genuinely human."

Part Three: Blessings Related to Church Buildings

Here one finds the rites of dedication for fonts of baptism, tabernacles, all sacred images and crosses, stations of the cross, and even the very doors of the building, which declare Christ to be the "gate," and that "whoever enters" through him "will be safe" (Jn 10:9).

The articles used in liturgical worship, the organ, and bells and holy water itself, all find their rites of blessing. Included as well is the Blessing of a Cemetery.

Part Four: Blessing of Religious Articles

Scapulars and rosaries, and other articles of devotion are blessed according to the rites in this portion of the Ritual, together with things connected with the honor given to the saints (Saint Anthony's Bread, etc.). Once again we find the value of the individual accorded rightful prominence. We are the Church, and individually live out the Church's life. Our worship, within the liturgy, is public worship, one that springs from the hearts of all who are involved. Private devotions are simply signs of that devotedness which the entire Church calls forth from those who follow her Lord.

Part Five: Various Blessings

As the title indicates, various other blessings are included here, especially rites of thankfulness. An appendix to this portion (as to the entire book) incorporates public periods of prayer (as during the rites for the dedication of a church.)

The Elements of Rites for Blessing

In the *Book of Blessings,* mandated by Vatican II, infused with its spirit of reverence for God's Word and openness to the world, the *Ritual* itself becomes a "sacramental" of how the Church speaks of God, and speaks of the world. In the language of official texts, approbations sought and received, rubrics, directives and the like, there is a wider dimension than the rites of blessing themselves. The *Ritual* bears promise, and, of course, promises can be kept or broken; this is why the very elements of these rites cannot be seen as matters that bear no weight.

1. Celebrations of the Community

The first characteristic of the rites of blessing, the book of festivities, if you will, is the notion that the entire community celebrates. As many as possible are encouraged to take part, not as a means of assuring a wider audience, but as an expression that it is the whole Church which worships. It is the entire community that expresses joy or consolation for the successes and failures of each member, and their use of things. Exceptions prove the rule, for there are situations when the number of participants must be limited, as when a sick person would otherwise be embarrassed or placed under stress by having many others present. That is a proper concern, a pastoral consideration, one that reflects a true reverence for persons.

Yet the basic truth stands: rites of blessing are not a purely individual matter, set free from their moorings in the human condition, and in the Church as a people somehow set apart. The communal aspect of the celebrations is reflected in the encouragement of as large a portion of the community as possible. It is reflected as well in the fact that the Word is proclaimed, presupposing a congregation, and in the wording of prayers, intercessions, song and gestures. The group reflects its wider dimensions, its sense of universal belonging, and the refusal to lessen the value inherent in things by confining any "blessing" to a single individual (even "grace" before a meal taken in solitude can be seen as a personal expression of how the entire assembly acts and gives thanks).

2. Priority of the Word of God

The *Book of Blessings* rightly joins word to deed, things said to things achieved. The Mass is seen as first centering around the Word, before focusing attention upon the saving and eucharistic deed; Sacraments are not celebrated apart from a liturgy of the Word. The rites of blessing reveal a similar twofold dimension, in which the Word of God is not simply read, but proclaimed, which involves catechesis and instruction. The word itself speaks, and so does the one who adds words of her or his own to say. The Word once spoken, and written down, is addressed to the present situation, to God's presence at the moment in hand.

Such proclamation does more than deepen or awaken faith. It provides the very meaning of what is taking place, and lends itself to that part of creation which is being celebrated. If some things are seen as no longer being "relevant," the Sacred Scriptures correct such a view. This approach of letting the Word of God, by which the world itself came to be, continue to speak to that world, is an ancient and continuing truth. The very thrust of Vatican II is the mode and manner of rediscovery.

3. Genuine Signs

Since sacramentals are "echoes" of "all that is genuinely human," they must be genuine in and of themselves. A history of the Church's perception of the "sacred" reveals a host of things wrongly perceived; the fault, however, lies in the perception. Truths wrongly perceived remained truths, even when not grasped completely. Superstitions did arise, and they will in years to come; no need to be surprised at this, but every need to be cautious without alarm.

Vestments became a place for symbols instead of a symbol; a gesture of peace, as we have seen, became a warning about the need to suffer, and led to a complete "theology" of Confirmation, which depleted meaning rather than adding to it. Perhaps, in the course of centuries, we have reversed the Cana event, and changed wine into water, and then stood back and spoke of a miracle.

Persons, places, times and things are authentic in and of themselves. A "sacramental" approach becomes authentic when the inherent nature is perceived and only then appreciated. In light of this, the next element has much to say.

4. The Blessing of God

It is this element that underlies the approach of the Hebrew Scriptures and New Testament, from the day when Abraham was told he "will be a blessing," and that "all the communities of the earth shall find blessing" in him (Gn 12:2,3), until the final scenes in scripture when blessings are given to the Almighty, and to the Lamb. "Blessed be Abram," Melchizedek declared, having added, "and blessed be God" (Gn 14:20,19). As Luke begins his story, he shows Zechariah saying, "Blessed be the Lord" while calling the events taking place, "the work of the kindness of our God" (Lk 1:68,78).

The rites of blessing establish the firm principle of creation: first, before time and place, and persons and things came to be, there is God. "Anyone who comes to God must believe that he exists" (Hb 11:6); the faith that perceives sacramentals affirms this basic truth, and the very form of the prayer of the Church, liturgy viewed as faith's expression, establishes this truth.

5. Formula of Blessing

Both the wording and the deed are encompassed by the term "formula," as though words were incomplete without deeds, somewhat like persons without one another. That words and gestures both have something to "say" does not mean that each speaks in a vacuum, or that both do not speak in concert. Each completes the other, and the new *Ritual* looks at the simple tracing of the cross, without Word and words, as incomplete, as something to be avoided, a void that cannot remain.

6. Intercessions

It is this element that speaks to the entire Body of Christ, identifying us with the one "who forever lives to make intercession" (Heb 7:25), and with his role as servant to the world, a task that belongs to the whole Christ, head and members.

The intercessions accomplish many purposes within the rites of blessing. They reaffirm the notion of the celebrations as communal, for all make intercession, minister and participants alike, and the entire community calls forth the blessing of God, even as it blesses God. They express faith, without which sacramentals are deprived of meaning. And they identify the community precisely as a cluster of servants, one with the world it is called to serve, even apart from the world's hearing.

Within the formula and the accompanying intercessions, the genuine signs *recall* the blessings that have accompanied a sacred history. They *declare*, in words and deeds, what the world declares. They *oblige*, even if only in recognition of our failure to serve. And they *foresee* the goal of service, a world restored, a making of "leather garments" in place of "fig leaves" sewn together.

7. Variety of Ministers

If the priority of God's Word within our worship, and the priority of an openness to the world, mark the revision of Catholic worship and life, this last element of the rites of blessing also establishes a priority — the task common to all the baptized, the priesthood of all believers. As has been the case, bishops, priests and deacons are seen as "entitled" to preside at the celebrations connected with "their ministry." Although a theology of ministry awaits its own development, the *Ritual* addresses itself to the ministry of all, even if the formulation is incomplete as of present.

The *what*, and *when*, and *where*, and *why*, and *how* of the rites of blessing are set forth; so, too, is the *who* that must be involved. It is this factor that can be seen as *mustard-seed*, with the attendant risk of a sesame seed, an irritant, or a grain of sand that makes walking increasingly difficult. For some, an end, for others, a beginning; for all, a present, both as gift and as moment.

The *Book of Blessings* sees women and men "entitled" to enact the blessings of the Church. Parents would bless their children, and preside at the blessing of an engaged couple.

Workers and technicians, the tools of their trade and expertise. Farmers and ranchers, their fields and livestock. The caring, their sick and befriended. Hosts, their guests. Teachers, their students. Those in ministry would bless catechists and eucharistic ministers, for example, that which is appropriate to duties accepted, and opportunities welcomed.

Bishops, priests and deacons preside at those blessings proper to their role, their duty. To be sure, there is still the caution of speaking in terms of others carrying out the rites when official ministers are "absent." We are speaking of mustard-seeds, after all, and not the full grown herb. But each seed carries with it the promise of tomorrows, and it is the tomorrow that is encapsuled in today that we can look at now.

CHAPTER XI

THE BLESSINGS YET TO COME

Having defined *sacramentals* as:

> The good of creation
> which the Church receives
> with thanksgiving
> made holy by God's Word and by prayer,
> which, like the sacraments they resemble,
> proclaim to the world
> the grace of redemption
> which transforms that world;

and having seen, in the elements of the rites of blessing, how definition has taken shape;
we come to examine two factors.
The first is the resemblance to sacraments, which is the proper realm in which persons are perceived and received. The second is the transformation of the world, those elements of our universe as perceived by persons.

Resemblance to Sacraments

"Almost every event" of our lives encounters the grace of

the Paschal Mystery; this is the teaching of the Constitution on the Sacred Liturgy (Art 61), reflecting the observation of St. Thomas Aquinas that the sacraments transform the strategic moments of human life, our rites of passage, as they are called. Taking place within a moment, sacraments are not entrapped by that moment. Like any moment, connected in time, there is a *before* and *after*, an *enduring* moment, even if seen only as celebrated *during* a moment. Sacramentals address this dimension. If they can be said to resemble the sacraments, it is because they bear semblance to this truth: sacraments are momentous, not simply moments.

Baptism

In the initiation of adult members of the community, the various stages of the catechumenate (the *before*) and post-baptismal instruction (the *after*) have regained their proper place in liturgy and life. The same may apply to human birth, which takes place at a moment in time, preceded and followed by times that are significant. Baptism (whether of infants or adults) can be seen within the perspective of birth and new life; at whatever moment baptism will take place, human life is seen as sacred, capable of being surrounded by sacramentals that resemble baptism.

— Pregnancy is more than an expectation of parents; it is an awaited time by the assembly of those who believe in life. The blessing before childbirth takes the parents' joy and makes it a cause for rejoicing by the community of which they are a part. Parents, grandparents and godparents (doctors and others as well) surround these months, and can be acknowledged by the rite of blessing.

— The rite of blessing parents at the close of the baptismal ceremony is one expression of a rite of thankfulness. Circumstances may dictate a separate blessing, what we once celebrated as the "churching" of mothers, which was, in essence and form, a rite of giving thanks. Rituals of "purification" or "churching" (separated from the church building, perceived in many cases as separation from the community) may have been perceived as such, but the rite always spoke of gratitude and blessing. This can be acknowledged by the community, who may well determine the proper minister of blessing.

— If the Lord proclaimed "blessed" those who are "sorrowful," the death of a child, the loss of a fetus, may also be "celebrated." We confront failures in our own lives, and failed hopes are proper cause for consolation by a concerned community.

— Other "rites of passage" can be similarly explored, for what speaks to one has something to say to all. That is the very nature of festival, applause and compensation for the lack of applause alike. Persons are to be celebrated, not their success alone; the heroic in Christian life is the dimension of faith preserved and expanded especially in life's most difficult moments, when surrender to God's sovereignty is heroic.

— The end of human life, already kept as "sacramental" in the rites of commendation and farewell, is not without its reference to Baptism; Paschal Candle and white cloth say this much. But the community has more than words to say, especially at a time when words are hard to find or determine. A blessing of those who know loss may well find its place in our ritual of life, especially when the loneliness sets in and seems to erase hope.

Confirmation

For many, this is perceived as a lost moment, a rite of fuller initiation seemingly out of place in the order in which other sacraments occur. For some, its only permanent mark is the "confirmation name" that was taken (or given) at the time. It is a "sealing" with the Holy Spirit that looks back, and looks forward, covering time in either direction.

— Some have suggested that Pentecost Sunday witnesses a renewal of Confirmation, just as Easter witnesses the renewal of baptismal promises. It is one way in which this sacrament can be rescued from oblivion. A similar "blessing" can easily become the "confirmation" of the Spirit's presence for those who have experienced a renewal of his power in their lives.

— In speaking of the Holy Spirit, Paul could say "the Spirit himself gives witness with our spirit that we are children of God" (Rom 8:16). Perhaps a rite of blessing could allow "the Spirit" and "our spirit" to join in appreciation of those who have witnessed, in their public lives, to the heroism of grace, and to the adherence to principle. As within the community, so within the larger community; as within Church, so within world. "The whole created world eagerly awaits," and "all creation groans" (Rom 8:19,22) its completion, its revelation. Why not a celebration of those within the Church, and those who are not members of the *ecclesia*, who have advanced the revelation, and drawn the world closer to its completion? Society gives its plaques and awards; cannot the Church bestow its blessing?

Reconciliation

All too often we tend to think in terms of a penitent's return, which is half a story at least. One can wonder whether the "younger" would have left his father's house had the "elder" not taken himself so seriously; we call it the parable of the Prodigal Son, but two brothers are involved, as well as two servants who often go unnoticed. Perhaps the day will return when the rites of reconciliation will become a rite of welcome to those who "left" us; if so, and the celebration does take place, there is reconciliation to take place in the one welcomed and the one who welcomes. Zaccheus climbed a tree because the crowd that followed Jesus gave him no opportunity to see the Lord. Salvation still came to his house, as the Lord looked above the crowd, and bid Zaccheus to come down. Parables have many meanings, and are stories for us to tell and retell.

The Church, while claiming to open doors to all, has often

been a place where estrangement was encountered. Perhaps our future will be bold enough to admit the fact, give it definition with rites of blessing, and offer some "sacramental" that grace perfects a fallen nature, even the Church's own nature.

Marriage

The new Ritual sees the celebration of anniversaries as completing the celebration of the sacrament of Marriage. These are occasions for joy, and have an impact beyond the couples themselves, their children, relatives and friends. The blessing of a home is but the sacramental of the blessings already within the home; the blessings of children, by their parents, or engaged couples by parents and in-laws, are sacramentals of blessings given and yet to be received. But there are other questions to ask.

Must the rites of blessing always be considered in the light of "authority" and responsibility alone? Cannot children bless their parents? Does this not convey an authority, if not a responsibility?

What about those whose marriages have broken? Or those who never married at all? Or those who could never have children? Rites of blessing, if they bear resemblance to the sacraments, can serve to spell out the significance of the sacrament in ways that are often neglected. If Matrimony is seen as a bond that bespeaks union of Christ and Church, can there not be rites of blessing which show that other states and situations do not deny such intimacy with the Lord?

Those in religious life, whose ceremony of profession has always been considered a sacramental, have been called to service. Their life is symbolic of our own; in community, they are a sign that we are the community of God; their prayers a reminder that we must "pray perseveringly " (Col 4:2). Theirs is a deepening of baptismal commitment, true, but a response given and made in love, the "other side of marriage," as some have called it. There are many "other sides," and the Sacrament of Marriage is enhanced, not lessened, by locating it within the entire context of human love which God's own love has intersected.

Holy Orders

Future ministries within the Church await their development within Church life and thought, but past ages have seen various ministries within the realm of sacramentals (sub-deacon, porter, exorcist, etc.) New ministries have emerged within the Church, and will continue to do so, as charisms and needs arise, and we come to perceive that we minister to the world.

The realm of Holy Orders does not coincide with the circle of ministries, but does fall within that circle; hopefully, in an ideal world, the circle of the Church's work will not even limit its ministerial function. But within the circle of the Church's life, rites of blessing, true celebrations of that life, will mark ministries begun, accepted and completed. If the designation of ministries is undertaken, and rites of blessing drawn up, they may bear semblance to the Sacrament of Orders as celebrations of the Church's call to be a servant.

This is not to speak in terms of "lay ministry," already seen as a redundancy, or of "appointing" members of the community, and "investing" them with rank, vesture and insignia. It is to say, however, that like ordinations, any rites of blessing connected with ministries are celebrations of what the Church is and is called to be — a reflection and continuation of him who "has not come to be served but to serve — to give his life in ransom for many" (Mk 11:45).

There is always the possibility for confusion of "orders" and authority. Any form of ministry can be fraught with the danger of turning service into disservice, and "clericalism" is not a term that need always betray its etymology. Yet, since ordinations celebrate the Church's priestly service, rites of blessing involving ministries can certainly be seen as bearing semblance to that fact.

Anointing

It is in this sacrament that the Church deals with sickness and health, with suffering and healing. The *Book of Blessings* envisions those involved with the care of the sick celebrating rites of blessing for the sick, for their very care is "sacramental" of healing. The Sacrament of Anointing affirms that those who are ill are a source of blessing, and that grace transforms and truly heals, in him who "bore our infirmities" (Is 53:4).

That same "Song of the Servant" speaks of him who was "spurned and avoided," and "held in no esteem" (Is 53:3). It is this aspect of human suffering that rites of blessing might address. A "stigma" is a mark of infamy, the dictionaries tell us, together with a further definition as referring to the wounds of Christ. The similarity exists without any need to consult a reference book.

Cannot future rites of blessing bear semblance to the Anointing by their attempt to heal? By their tacit recognition of Pascal's observation that *"Christ sera en agonie jusqu'au fin du temps"*? Are the gospels not able to be heard anew when we realize that "there is one among you whom you do not recognize" (Jn 1:26)?

One looks with admiration at Alcoholics Anonymous, Al-Anon, and similar organizations. The *Book of Blessings*, seeking to support "every good endeavor" of civil society, offers a blessing upon organizations devoted to public safety (fire departments, and such). Could not future rites praise those who support those bearing a stigma, and in need of support?

The *Ritual* envisions a blessing of pilgrims and travelers. Could not future rites enjoin a blessing upon those who are a blessing to the homeless, the hungry, the naked, the imprisoned and the stranger? Do not these same groups receive the "Father's blessing," as they stand before the "Son of Man," and receive praise for what they did to the "least" of Christ's sisters and brothers (Cf. Mt 25:31-46)? Or must we wait for parable to become reality at the last day?

EPILOGUE:

In its appreciation of persons, in its designation of ministers, and in its establishing of priorities, the *Book of Blessings* marks a true beginning, while showing itself careful of interpreting the past and of remaining faithful to the traditions from which it sprang. Its appearance is applauded, yet it suggests that further questions be asked. In its appreciation of the role of persons as sacramentals, as having meaning beyond that which all persons have, it promotes the truth of Vatican II: "The Council lays stress on respect for the human person: everyone should look upon one's neighbor (without any exception) as another self" (*Gaudium et Spes*, Art 27).

A World Transformed

The Constitution on the Sacred Liturgy took note that "scarcely any proper use of material things ... cannot be directed toward the sanctification of persons and the praise of God" (Art 61). That statement is but the other side of what the Council declared in *Gaudium et Spes*: "By the very nature of creation, material being is endowed with its own stability, truth and excellence" (Art 36).

The God, whom the scriptures reveal as favoring so many persons, inspired them to bless him for the abundance and "excellence" of his creation. As with the leather garments that God had fashioned in Eden, those whom he favored saw in the things of earth signs of his favor, and reassurances of his covenant. The rites of blessing declare the "truth and excellence" of creation; they are directed to the "praise of God" and human "sanctification." In other words, creation is received as gift, the Giver of all gifts being acknowledged thereby, and the use of such gifts viewed as more than simple usage, but having a role in our own development as daughters and sons of God. The "proper use" of material things has a usefulness within the realm of faith.

Things blessed *recall* their origin. They *declare* their own excellence, and faith declares them more excellent still. They *oblige* us to make use of them to acknowledge that "the things of the world and the things of faith derive from the same God" (*Gaudium et Spes*, Art 36). And they *foresee* the day that is to come:

> "When we have spread on earth the fruits of our nature and our enterprise — human dignity, brotherly communion and freedom — according to the command of the Lord and his Spirit, we will find them once again ... illuminated and transfigured. ... here on earth the kingdom is mysteriously present" (*Gaudium et Spes*, Art 39).

The sacramentals are rightly seen as signs of a redeemed creation, in which human labor and life, making proper use of created things, so accept the "truth and excellence" of the world as to declare and promote the greater truth and excellence that is faith. It sees material things intimately connected with the human person, achieving even greater value in their service to persons, especially when personhood reaches heights of fulfillment in faith.

There is always the danger that the things of creation, correctly seen as values, will be mistaken for ends. We are to "be intent on things above rather than on things of earth" (Col 3:2), but we are not to "view things superficially" (2 Cor 10:7). The things of earth call attention to the things above and are revealed in them. One cannot be content with earthly things, and intent upon the heavenly. There is something of a tension between the two, and that tension is resolved by the proper use of things. Or, as the Church prays:

> God our Father,
> open our eyes to see your hand at work
> in the splendor of creation,
> in the beauty of human life.
> Touched by your hand our world is holy.
> Help us to cherish the gifts that surround us,
> to share your blessings with our brothers and sisters,
> and to experience the joy of life in your presence.

The tension between "things of earth" and "things above" finds its resolution in the simple conjunction, "and." It is not a question of *either/or*, but a question of *both/and*. Touched by our own hands, this holy world is also transformed, cherished, and like all things cherished, shared. Such an approach, truly Catholic, truly "universal," is evident in the rites of blessings, which provide celebration, and point to the lack of celebration as well; they look to those who "have," with an eye upon those who "have not;" they recognize "splendor" in creation, and seek to foster the "beauty" that human life must be allowed to be.

Small Symbol of a Large World Transformed

If the world can be seen as transformed, and filled with mystery, Catholic devotional life has made use of one particular item that symbolizes such an outlook — the Rosary. It has been an article of devotion traditionally taken as an identifying mark of one's Catholic faith, the gift given at important moments in life, the item held by people of every walk of life, and even placed in the coffin to reveal that mysteries once pondered are mysteries no longer.

Legends have abounded concerning the origins of the rosary. Held in such high esteem, it was deemed an actual revelation from God, or a gift of the Virgin to one of her devoted children, such as Saint Dominic.

In point of fact, its origins lie unknown to us, and its history reveals a development, so that many rosaries have come to exist. We understand the term to refer to a string of beads, and to three sets of mysteries — Joyful, Sorrowful and Glorious. When all the mysteries have been pondered, the sum of "Aves" totals one-hundred-and-fifty, the number of Psalms in the Bible.

The *Ave Maria*, recapturing the very moment of the Incarnation, came to be seen as the "poor person's Psalm." It summed up the Psalter, seen as a compilation of hymns of expectancy that found their fulfillment when Christ was born. To the unlettered, to those who could not read the

Bible simply because copies did not exist in large numbers, and those that did were to be found in churches and monasteries, the Rosary became the "psalter" of ordinary folk.

There is a sense of totality about this popular article of devotion. Like Paul's famous hymn (Phil 2:6-11), which sums up the Incarnation, the mysteries trace the events of Christ's life — before, during and after his earthly existence among us. The joy of his coming, the sorrow over his sufferings and death, and the glory of his resurrection, a glory shared by those who believe in him, are all present to the one who prays.

The mystery of Christ's coming to us, heaven's plan being realized by the assent of a daughter of the earth, was and will be a source of wonder and awe. As though to capture mystery, and make it something one can handle, the use of beads suited the task admirably. To the imagination's eye, one can see worlds of mystery in the small spheres upon which fingers move. The immanent made transcendent; the mind moving in unison with the body; prayer caught up with action: these lie at the heart of the recitation of psalter-prayers, prayers that have, at their very center, the name of Jesus.

Here our hands are "at work" as we ponder God's "hand at work in the splendor of creation," and "in the beauty of human life," especially that beauty which is found in the humanity of Jesus, the "fruit" of Mary's womb.

In the blessing of articles of devotion, as in the rites used to dedicate her churches and their furnishings, the Church admits that the sacred is of this world. At the same time, in her blessings of the things of earth considered "profane," the tools and activities of all humankind, the Church admits that the world is of the sacred.

Benedictiones Ad Omnia

In the former Ritual, there was a *Benedictio Ad Omnia*, a "blessing of anything," jokingly referred to as "a blessing of whatever." It spoke of the elements that are essential to the

Church's rites: God's word, which makes all things holy; the use of anything to serve the will of God; the invocation of his holy name; the request for God's protection; and lastly, the seeking of God's gifts for soul and body.

Such a blessing was more than a mere afterthought; if anything it *foresaw* the development of art and science and every endeavor that moves the human spirit to marvel and stand in awe, and to play as a child upon the earth. It looked at the holiness inherent in a world which the redemption is creating anew. It places the Creator above the creature after all, and the human creature, with its excellences and flaws, as fully human only when faith has deepened our ability to reason and speak and move.

By way of afterthought, yet not precisely as such, the final "blessing" of the former Ritual still offers a capacity for us to enlarge our vision. There is a wider circle to the realm of "sacramentals" than those which a Book of Blessings can contain. That is the personal world of every member of the community we call the Church. As we have seen, much that was purely private and personal lent itself to the entire Church, as in the case of the Liturgy of the Hours, borrowed from the prayers of individual Christians who went to their "room," closed their "doors," and prayed "to the Father in private" (Dt 6:6).

The Lord who commanded us to pray in secret also went to the synagogue "as he was in the habit of doing"(Lk 4:16). The one never excludes the other. In the Catholic tradition, public worship cannot sum up all the prayers and adoration of our lives. And sacramentals selected by the Church cannot adequately exhaust all that is sacred in our lives. There is much that arises spontaneously, limited only by a lack of imagination.

Each of us has a particular place within our homes that is favored for prayer and pondering, whether an entire room, or a portion of that room. Each of us selects a time not otherwise given to other functions, and they can change, no less sacred when shifted from morning to evening or dead of night. Not one of us is without that gesture which instinctively arises as the mind and heart are uplifted in the presence of our God.

These are the *benedictiones ad omnia*. They include such things as this modest work has overlooked, and things which this or any other work could hardly know, except to know that they do exist for us. Each of us has our own "sacramentals." They are persons, places, times and things, and everything else besides. They form the material for our own unwritten book of blessing, the ancient "blessing of whatever."

And that's as good a word as any with which to conclude. Whatever.

EPILOGUE/PROLOGUE

In the last century, as inventiveness and progress continued to mark the Industrial Revolution, and startling changes continued to shake the world, Charles Kingsley felt the need to state:

> "Give me the political economist, the sanitary reformer, the engineer, and take your saints and virgins, relics and miracles. The spinning-jenny and the railroad, Cunard's liners and the electric telegraph, are to me ... signs that we are, on some points at least, in harmony with the universe" (*Yeast*, Ch. 5, written in 1848).

There is a fatal flaw in Kingsley's argument, and that flaw is itself a sign of how sinfulness has marred our vision. The flaw lies not with the world itself, but with our perception of that world. There are not two worlds, the sacred and the profane, but one.

What Kingsley saw as miracles are themselves "relics" now, confined to museums for the curious, or to photographs in history books. Our world today is one of microchips and lasers, supersonic transports and shuttle spacecraft, and one day these will be "relics" of a bygone era. Meanwhile, the Church will have its saints and virgins, its relics and miracles still.

Had Kingsley ever stood in the central square of Nuremberg, opposite the Marienkirché, and gazed upon the magnificent fountain that still delights the visitor, he might have seen things differently. The fountain is an elaborate tower, with four sides to mark the compass-points. It is peopled with the great figures of human history, those who have enlightened the world, and tapped its wisdom.

David is seated not very far from Dante, and Paul can look across at Plato. At the very top one finds Mark and Matthew and Luke and John. Economists and prophets, engineers and saints, representative of all the world's wisdom, cluster around the tower, each with a symbol of that art or science whereby that person towered above so many others.

There may appear to be a world of difference between "the political economist" and "the saint," or between "the engineer" and "the virgin," but there is not. Life is an art and a science both, and life in Christ is no less so. Faith, like life, is a gift, and both are meant to be lived. Faith, like any talent, is a gift, and both are intended for use. Faith perfects reason in much the same way that grace perfects nature.

David and Aristotle have every right to appear together in a public square, as at Nuremberg, and both are seated properly beneath the high artistry of the evangelists.

Perhaps there is greater symbolism than intended in our *Book of Blessings*. It offers a rite for the "Blessing of Bridges." Sacramentals do bridge a world that might otherwise seem worlds apart. So we'll take the reformers and economists together with the saints and virgins; and we'll take the modern spinning-jenny, and the counterparts to railroads and telegraphs, together with our saints and virgins, those of the past and those yet to be revealed.

In one particular saint and virgin, by whom countless artists were inspired, we might see that view of the world in which the sacred and the profane are one. Art has sought to capture the significance of this woman, and have used canvas and marble and music to depict what Luke portrayed with his pen.

Her very title, "Mother of God," bridges the realms of earth and heaven. Catholic tradition has reveled in its fascination with her, the woman we call "blessed." We do so not only because her *Magnificat* declares that "all generations" would do so (Lk 1:48), but because she herself is a sacramental of what it means to be "blessed."

Her very "being" proclaimed "the greatness of the Lord" (Lk 1:46), as does everything that has being. Upon learning her name, "Mary," we then learn her role; she is the "highly favored daughter," and "blessed among women" (Lk 1:28, 29). But there is more to learn. As the story of the Incarnation continues to unfold, we find her saying: "I am the servant of the Lord. Let it be done to me as you say." And at that, "the angel left her" (Lk 1:38).

It is right for angels to depart at this point, for two worlds have merged, now, and the "seen and unseen" have blended at the word of their Creator.

Within the mystery of that moment, from which so many lessons can be drawn, the very nature of sacramentals emerges. Mary can be taken to represent every "highly favored daughter," each called to "proclaim the greatness of the Lord." The Church can rightly summon the realities of earth and command from them the realities of heaven. What is seen has greater depths from which the unseen can be allowed to have its say. With an excellence that was already hers, she gained a nobler state — "servant of the Lord."

In a world of sacraments and sacramentals, where the Incarnation is accepted and affirmed, and where the human constantly interacts with the divine, the hidden is unveiled. Precisely where the divine and the human meet and merge do we come to an understanding (however partial) of the mystery that is God, and of God's ways with his daughters and sons.

In their own spheres, the arts and sciences are "highly favored daughters." When put at the service of God, they "let it be done" as he says. Thus, within the Church, is the poet allowed to speak his words, the scientist able to disclose what she unlocked, and every art and science, like every person, given to reveal what lies hidden — a world, a creation, a transfiguration.

The one who distrusts the world of metaphor and analogy

mistrusts the world as it is at its very center. And at times such lack of trust is understandable. There does exist within our world sin and pain and suffering; but there is also reconciliation and healing with joy. In *Catholicism*, Henri de Lubac warned that "the Christian is not given the privilege of strolling across the battlefield sniffing a rose."

But the Christian is given a privilege — that of knowing that the battlefields were once places where roses grew, and where they must grow once again. To see battlefields does not excuse one from claiming fields of flowers. There is sadness, but there is goodness as well, and that is the proper realm of the sacramentals.

There is sadness, and there is goodness, whenever bread is broken and wine is poured. There was a sadness and a goodness when Body was broken by death, and Blood flowed from wounded side. Yet the sacramental view insists that the Friday of Christ's death be termed "Good."

In the final analysis, we must hold that sacramentals are by no means insignificant, any more than Bethlehem was. What Micah called "too small to be among the clans of Judah" (Mi 5:1) became a city that grew at the moment of the Incarnation, termed "by no means least among the princes of Judah" (Mt 2:6).

Creation is being redeemed, enlarged beyond merely human perception. That is the truth which sacramentals declare, and why an "afterword" is hardly that at all. Epilogue is Prologue, and such is the very nature of things.

Recommended Reading

The Bible and the Liturgy. Jean Daniélou. University of Notre Dame Press, Notre Dame, 1966.

The Earth is the Lord's. A.J. Heschel. World Publishing Co., Cleveland, 1963.

Elements of Rite. Aidan Kavanagh. Pueblo Publishing Co., New York, 1982.

Environment and Art in Catholic Worship. The Bishops Committee on the Liturgy. United States Catholic Conference, Washington, 1978.

Fundamentals of the Liturgy. John H. Miller, C.S.C. Fides Publishers, Notre Dame, 1964.

Holy Places, Journal of the Liturgical Conference, Vol. 3, No. 4, The Liturgical Conference, Washington, 1983.

Images and Symbols. Mircea Eliade. Sheed and Ward, New York, 1969.

Introduction to Christian Worship. James F. White. Abingdon Press, Nashville, 1982.

Parable of Community. Roger Schutz. Seabury, New York, 1981.

Prayer. Abhishiktanada (Henri le Saux, O.S.B.). Westminster, Philadelphia, 1973.

Riches Despised. Conrad Pepler. Herder, St. Louis, 1957.

The Sabbath, Its Meaning for Modern Man. A.J. Heschel. Farrar, Straus and Giroux, New York, 1983.

Sacred Signs. Romano Guardini. Michael Glazier, Inc., Wilmington, 1979.

Sanctifying Life, Time and Space. Marion Hatchett. Seabury, New York, 1976.

A Short History of the Western Liturgy. 2nd. ed. Theodor Klauser, Oxford University Press, London, 1979.

Theological Dimensions of the Liturgy. Cyprian Vagaggini, O.S.B. The Liturgical Press, Collegeville, 1976.

Towards a Renewal of Sacramental Theology. Raymond Vaillancourt. Matthew J. O'Connell, Trans. The Liturgical Press, Collegeville, 1979.

Vatican Council II, The Conciliar and Post-Conciliar Documents. Austin Flannery, O.P., Gen. Ed. Costello Publishing, Northport, 1980.